Horace Wilbert Bolton

Our Fallen Heroes, and Other Addresses

Horace Wilbert Bolton

Our Fallen Heroes, and Other Addresses

ISBN/EAN: 9783337213947

Printed in Europe, USA, Canada, Australia, Japan

Cover: Foto ©ninafisch / pixelio.de

More available books at **www.hansebooks.com**

Yours sincerely
H. W. Bolton

OUR FALLEN HEROES

AND OTHER ADDRESSES

BY

H. W. BOLTON,

AUTHOR OF

"Home and Social Life" — "The Soul's Cry" —
"Patriotism" — "Our Fallen Heroes" —
"Reminiscences of the War" and
"America's Next War."

PUBLISHED BY
H. W. BOLTON,
409 West Monroe Street,
CHICAGO, ILL.

TO
THE LOVERS AND DEFENDERS OF OUR COUNTRY,
This volume is respectfully dedicated
BY THE AUTHOR.

Entered, according to Act of Congress, in the year 1892,
BY HORACE W. BOLTON,
In the Office of the Librarian of Congress at Washington.

PREFACE.

The lectures which constitute this volume were delivered before patriotic organizations, from time to time, with no thought of publishing them, as the field seemed so well supplied with patriotic literature.

And I was slow to believe that there was room for a contribution of mine. But being urged to give them in book form to the public, I yielded to the advice of friends and published the most of them in my work called PATRIOTISM, which is now out of print.

With this explanation, I send this volume forth with a prayer that it may awaken a deeper and stronger love for the land in which we live, and for the preservation of which so much blood and treasure have been expended.

H. W. BOLTON.

INTRODUCTION.

I have read with great profit the addresses embodied in this volume, and, after perusing them, felt as one of the millions who in 1861-65 showed their love for liberty and country. Every young man especially, whether native or foreign born, should read patriotic utterances, since otherwise he is apt to become indifferent to the institutions to which he is indebted for the freedom he enjoys. The perpetuity of the Union depends upon the instruction given the young, for if inculcated in youth, patriotism will control the actions of manhood, in the event of peril to the Nation. The graphic account of what was accomplished by the soldiers of the Republic; their trials and tribulations; the long and weary marches; the exposure to heat and cold; the hard-fought battles, cannot fail to be interesting to those who were active participants in the war for the preservation of the Government that it might be handed down unimpaired to future generations and left to their intelligent and watchful care. The fact should not be overlooked that a large part of our present population was born since the surrender at Appomattox. Their eyes never beheld the Stars and Stripes until after the christening with the blood of our dead comrades, who sacrificed their lives as evidence that the flag really symbolized "Liberty to all men." Another large portion of the people, numbering millions, has come from foreign lands since 1865. It is the duty, therefore, of all in a position to do so, to instil into their minds sentiments of loyalty to the Government which shelters and protects them, and affords them the same opportunities in the race of life that are accorded the native citizen.

My prayer is that the God of the living and the dead may bless your efforts to foster the spirit of patriotism, and thus aid in the continuance of the grandest Republic on the face of the earth.

Yours in F. C. and L.,

JAMES A. SEXTON.

CONTENTS.

CHAPTER.		PAGE.
I.	CENTENNIAL	9
II.	FALLEN HEROES	34
III.	GENERAL GRANT	56
IV.	GENERAL LOGAN	74
V.	GENERAL SHERIDAN	90
VI.	GENERAL CROOK	109
VII.	SOLDIERS' ATTITUDE	125
VIII.	GENERAL SHERMAN	145
IX.	GENERAL SHERMAN, BY GENERAL O. O. HOWARD	167
X.	WISDOM AND WAR, BY REV. DR. GEORGE H. COREY	177

And yet there's another country, still vaster than all these;
Encrowned by lofty mountain chains, and washed by mighty
    seas;
No bigotry of worship holds her conscience in duress,
No mystery veils her altars, no censor curbs her press;
With her women of the fairest that bloom beneath the sky,
With her soldiers of the boldest that ever dared to die,
With her flag, in glory, spreading o'er the earth and o'er the
    sea.
Like a portent to the tyrant, like a rainbow to the free;
With the nations flowing toward her, as to a promised rest—
This, this, of all the lands I saw, is the land I love the best.
                                            —*Everhart.*

PATRIOTISM.

CHAPTER I.

CENTENNIAL ADDRESS.*

This is an eventful hour in the history of a great nation—a moment, into which is crowded an hundred years of constitutional life, with success sufficient to demand the suspension of business, the ringing of bells, the booming of cannon, the chanting of choirs, and the best efforts of the public speaker.

We meet as Americans and patriots, sixty million strong, to unfurl the stars and stripes over a blossoming earth and beneath a smiling heaven. To us this flag is the emblem of liberty, equal rights and national unity.

As patriots we have reason, on this fourth day of July, 1889, to rejoice, and to make some public demonstration of our love of native land. Great love for native land is strong among all nations, even causing the natives of Asiatic islands, on beholding a banana tree in the public gardens of Paris to be so

---

*Delivered at Aurora, Ill., July 4, 1889.

stirred as to baptize the plant with tears; and even the Esquimaux becomes so wedded to the frigid zone of his native land as to think the blubber and ice cabin preferable to the gifts of more enlightened nations and refined society. But why does the heart so tenaciously cling to that spot on earth where first it learned to live? And we answer, it is because of the friendships and blessings which were all the world to us. But true patriotism is more than that, for there are and always have been, true patriots who were born on other shores.

The nations waited for the history of our own country to develop the patriotism that should make the sons of all climes and all lands one in defence of the institutions of a free republic.

We go not back into ancient history for illustrations of true patriotism. Tell us not of the Persian invaders who entered Greece. Speak not to-day of the heroism displayed at Marathon, for we have heard of Bunker Hill, Lexington, Princeton, Shiloh, Fair Oaks, Gettysburg, Lookout Mountain and Richmond We have read of, and learned to admire, the spirit of patriotism displayed during the war of the Rebellion by the gunner Wood, on board the Cumberland, while in combat with the Merrimac in Chesapeake Bay, who, having lost both legs and arms, and being offered assistance, as his ship was going down with her flag still flying, cried out: "Back to your guns, boys; give 'em fits! Hurrah for the flag!" We have seen more than a half-million men leave the shops, mines and schools of our land to fight for the maintenance of liberty and equal rights, believing that our only safety was in unity; and in the spirit of Washington, have watched with jealous anxiety the union of the States, believing it to be of infinite moment, discountenancing every suspicion or suggestion of division. In the days of Abraham Lincoln, being citizens by birth and by adoption, we said, "Amen," to his proclamation, and went forth to save the Union, "Constitution or no Constitution."

We glory in the spirit of Lieut. Cummings, who, while gliding up the Mississippi river and passing the Vicksburg batteries, had one leg torn from him by a rebel ball, but refused help, and said, "Get the ship past the batteries, boys, and they can have the other leg if they want it." Such is the patriotism of American history.

In the fiery furnace of war men have learned to love this their native and adopted home more than all others. Yes, the stubborn Englishman, the heroic Scotchman, the enthusiastic Irishman, the hearty German and the fun-loving Frenchman join in singing:

> My country, 'tis of thee,
> Sweet land of liberty,
>   Of thee I sing
> Land where my fathers died;
> Land of the Pilgrims' pride;
> From every mountain side
>   Let Freedom ring.

There are good reasons for the strength of our patriotism. This is a home-land; a land in which all may find protection in the exercise of a good conscience. Territorially we have room for all who desire to come and share with us. Should China and India conclude to move over with their seven hundred millions, we need have no fear.

We leave the first centennial round of the ladder of progress, with a population of more than sixty millions, thus ranking among the first nations on the globe. In less than a century we may lead all. Our population is at least twenty times as great as it was one hundred years ago; but of course we cannot calculate upon the same rate of increase for the next century.

Relatively, there will be a decrease in the number of immigrants, as it is quite probable that the spirit of enterprise or the love of adventure will carry away the successors of our frontier population to Africa and South America, as the continents of the future.

At the present rate of increase our population in the year 2000 will exceed eight hundred millions; but if the lowest estimates are used as a basis for calculation, the beginning of the twenty-first century will show an aggregate population of about two hundred and eighty millions.

Whether so vast a population can be sustained within our present limits is a problem for the future; but for one I entertain no doubt that the sustaining power of the United States will be adequate to the support of a population of one billion, without any impairment of the enjoyments and comforts of social and domestic life.

If we assume that the habitable area of the states is two million, five hundred thousand square miles, an average population of three hundred to the square mile would give an aggregate of seven hundred and fifty million souls.

Our capacity may be further measured by considering the fact that if the present inhabitants of the United States could be transferred to Texas, the average would not exceed three hundred persons to the square mile.

These facts do not in any way measure or limit the possibilities of comfortable existence, for this reason: The diversity of human pursuits, due to science, art and a wise public policy, is making a constant and appreciable addition to the capacity of the country to sustain human life.

The sixty millions within our borders are better fed, better clothed and better housed than were the three millions who inaugurated the Revolutionary war. It is not improbable that this progress may continue for a long and indefinite period. We have thus in one hundred years rushed to the foremost rank in population, wealth and annual savings; and we leave behind the nations of the earth on this our centennial celebration. Nearly as many English-speaking people dwell on these shores as in all the world beside. In public credit, in agriculture and manufactures, America leads the civilized world. Her territory is not half occupied.

To-day we have in wealth forty-five billions, and our annual manufactures amount to one billion, one hundred and twelve million pounds sterling, or nearly half as much as all Europe.

Float on, our flag! Beneath thy folds the wealth of numberless millions awaits the coming of unborn generations.

Again, this rapid growth does not endanger the nation's wealth, for God has stored in the hills and along the prairies immeasurable wealth in crude forms. Two hundred years have just consumed the underbrush, while the grand old forests of timber remain growing faster to-day than we cut and burn.

The lead, zinc, copper, tin, silver and gold are but a matter of search: the best and largest quantities are not yet reached. The materials for quarrying, smelting and coining are still in large quantities. The sunshine of other days, when beast and bird occupied the land, is now buried in Pennsylvania, Mississippi and Arkansas in 160,000 square miles of condensed light and power, and God hath in these last days shown us how to set the current on fire all about us.

Drive on, ye men of thought! Build your magazines, harness the steeds of the sky. We have minerals and power sufficient to make this nation the city of gold, with pearly gates and foundations of precious stones.

Our freightage surpasses that of Great Britain, France and Italy. Pennsylvania, with her railroad system, transports more tonnage than all Great Britain's merchant ships. And yet there is a demand for more railroads to do the work of that State.

Our flag floats over a land that is more beautiful than any other. Behold her rivers, placid and turbulent, threading the prairies of the West. What other land has a city like Chicago, a thousand miles inland, with wharves where ships from all parts of the earth may lie. Thus described: "I have been in Chicago six weeks. I shall take a look at it after awhile, when this feeling of stupidity, produced by amazement, partially wears off. But I shall not describe it. I am not writing books just now. If the Palace hotel, the Flood building, the new Chronicle building, the Baldwin, the Nevada block and all the palaces on Nob Hill were suddenly lifted up and set down in the midst of Chicago in one night, they would not be noticed next morning—unless they were set down in the middle of the streets, so as to interfere with traffic. Miles and miles of Flood buildings, groups of Baldwin theatres, townfuls of Nob Hill palaces, whole streets of new Chronicle buildings, innumerable Occidental hotels, all the elegant dry goods stores of San Francisco merged into one and then reduplicated till you are weary; all its restaurants rolled into one and multiplied until you are faint; cable cars going in trains like steam cars, with three conductors on each train; four elevators in a group, and no use ringing, because one or two are constantly ready to carry you up, or bring you down; morning papers, noon papers, evening papers and extras at midnight: a hundred miles of asphalt driveways for pleasure; innumerable streets, so long and brilliantly lighted that, standing at any point on one of them at night, you will see the parallel rows of lights come to a point in either direction, making the street look like a long, narrow diamond; granite, marble, brass, glass, colored crystals, electric lights, gorgeousness, brilliance, luxuriousness, magnificence-Chicago." A ship starting from New Orleans and going up the Mississippi and through her tributaries will sail more miles, and go through a greater variety of scenery, with more that is truly beautiful, than is found in a voyage around the globe.

Fly over this grand western world, and look on acres in rolling splendor, voiced with vegetation that blooms and blossoms like the rose.

Then turn to your mountain peaks, where eternal snows crown their slopes, and ice jewels their brows, and Switzerland will grow insipid and small. She might sit in all her Alpine splendor in the lap of Pennsylvania, as a toy for her children.

Then through your valleys hasten east over mighty lakes, to see the granite hills and mountains, scattered by an Omnipotent hand, to beautify the landscape, and for the use of man.

Friends, tell me not of scenes of beauty beyond the ocean, until I have seen the mountains and valleys of New England, the western prairies, the southern valleys and Pacific slopes.

Tell me not of Africa's coral-bound shores until I shall have seen our own mountains put on their autumn robes and snow-white crowns, or shall have breathed the balm of Florida's groves.

This flag is the emblem of freedom. We are a free people, and no intelligent man lives among us who will attempt to defend a system of slavery of any kind.

A well-known judge, attempting to convince a fugitive slave that he had made a mistake, put the following questions to him: "What did you run away for?" "Well, judge, I wanted to be free." "You had a bad master, I suppose?" "Oh, no, berry good mas'r." "Well you hadn't a good home?" "Hadn't I? You should see my pretty cabin in Kentucky." "Had to work hard, then?" "Oh, no, fair day's work." "Well, then, if you had plenty to eat, was not overworked, had a good home, I don't see what on earth you wanted to run away for." "Well, Massa Judge, I 'spect the situation am still open, if yo' would like it."

The judge did not apply for the position, but became a convert to abolition, and gave the fugitive a five dollar bill, to help him on his way to the land of freedom.

> "Up, all who strike for Freedom's cause!
> Send forth the thrilling battle cry;
> Quick to the fight—no time to pause—
> The choice is death or victory;
> Give freedom to the toiling slave,
> Or sleep within a warrior's grave."

Thank God for the songs of freedom!

Again, this is a land of schools and churches. A man cannot escape their influence if he would. As soon as a mother can trust her boy from her presence, the bell calls him to school. One hundred and ninety-eight thousand eight hundred and eighty-four schools open their doors to all classes of all nationalities, at an expense of $74,400,000 annually, and the land is flooded with aids to progress. Our publications are literally beyond computation, and the educational influences of the day are covering the hills with blessings all divine.

Equality! Once enrolled as a citizen of this country, we may go forth hoping to win any position in the gift of the nation, with ten thousand agencies awaiting our coming, which offer their unsought council and energy to urge us on our way. With us success is privileged. The humblest child from the most obscure home under the flag of our Union has an equal right to that patronage which should make him great among men. Of us Lord Bacon spoke when he said: "It remaineth for God and angels to be lookers on." For in an American race every man has a right to lead and a chance to rule. Birth and age are ruled out. Votes bring in.

The slab houses of the East and the log huts of the West are still honored, for out from these come the boys with convictions and a mother's blessing, to take the positions of honor and trust. We look back on the men whom we have honored, and we speak of Washington, not as a scholar, but as a man of force and will such as gave him character and standing; of Jackson as the fighter who overruled a mother's wish, for she desired that he should preach. He would not, but fight he would, and, passing through the darkness of 1813, he lived on hickory nuts, and would not die uncrowned. Had he failed in his election, with the old Jews I should be tempted to seek his grave, as they sought John's, to see if the earth still moved over him, and if he still expected to be President.

Abraham Lincoln, of our own State, rose to shake off the snow that sifted through the chinks of his father's cabin, and became the honored head of this great nation. He stirs our hearts to-day as do few men in American history.

What shall we say of our peerless Grant, our scholarly Sumner, able Greeley, heroic Garfield, brave and patriotic Sherman, Logan and Sheridan, and a long list of other noble men, whose names are interwoven with the history of our country?

None of them had opportunity such as is offered to the average son of '89, but, entering into life to employ the trinity of manhood and the indomitable energy of the true American, they were bound to rise by force of their own character.

This is emphatically a land of industry. Without work we cannot succeed. It matters not so much what a man does, so long as it be legitimate employment and is well done. Here this lesson is taught as under no other form of government.

Go visit the halls, look on the orchestra. What part is most essential? The leading violinist, who with his nimbleness attracts most attention or the director who with baton in hand gives direction to rhythm and expression? What of that man swinging those heavy sticks and beating that unsightly drum? Is he of no importance? Certainly he is. He marks the time, gives character and support to the melody, and is indispensable to the orchestra.

So in life, we are often more interested and give most attention to those preparing for the pulpit or for the practice of law, or medicine. Heaven knows we need a better class of lawyers, doctors and ministers, but that is not enough. We need better producers and more of them.

If the principles of the fathers be maintained and the loyalty of the sons continue, the old flag is yet to float over wealth, honor and beauty such as history has never known.

Therefore it becomes the true patriot to know of the dangers as well as the glories of his home land.

What are the dangers that threaten the American republic most?

I should place as chief among the foes that of wealth.

I see vastly more danger from our wealth than from our poverty. Mr. Webster once said, after traveling through the vast territory of the West: "I see before us abundance, luxury, decay and dissolution."

It requires no great study of history to see that abundance leads to luxury and extravagance, and that extravagance begets recklessness, idleness and vice. It was so with Greece and Rome. In the days of Marcus Aurelius Rome became very wealthy, and increased in riches until any governor could make himself rich in a year, but they spent their money in a way that led to vice, until the kingdom became corrupt, and died of its own shame.

Our wealth is becoming so great as to attract the attention of the whole world. Our gold and silver mines produce $100,000,000 annually; other mines and factories, $500,000,000; while our railroads add $250,000,000, and the agricultural interests more than $7,256,000,000.

Every sunrise adds $25,000,000 to our wealth as a nation, and men who love money are hastening to our shores, where the opportunity for wealth exists.

It is said on good authority that we have wealth in our soil this side of Alaska sufficient to feed 900,000,000 people, and then export 5,000,000,000 bushels of grain annually.

Then we turn our thoughts to the wealth under

the soil. Between 1870 and 1880 our product in precious metals amounted to $732,000,000. The United States furnishes more than one-half of the gold and silver of to-day, and it is not unreasonable to expect that our agricultural resources alone, when fully developed, will be capable of feeding two billions of people. Truly has Matthew Arnold said: "America holds the future." These facts are truly wonderful. Our property is valued at more than $50,000,000,000—more than enough to buy the Russian or the Turkish empire, and the kingdoms of Sweden and Norway, Denmark and Italy, together with Australia. Great Britain is by far the richest nation of the Old World, and yet our wealth exceeds hers by over $5,000,000 000. This is found in material the quantity of which may be multiplied by hundreds of millions. Well may Mr. Gladstone say, "The United States will probably become the head servant and the great household of the world, the employer of the employed, because her servants will be the most and ablest."

These facts are not calculated to win or entice the best class of society. The immigration of the last decade is not what it was thirty or forty years ago. Then they came to our country to find a home where liberty and freedom from religious restraints and persecutions were promised. They came with prayer and hymn-books. As when Columbus, first touching the soil, with cross in hand, knelt to kiss the earth and offer praise unto God, so the Pilgrims of

Plymouth Rock walked on their knees for months in devout reverence before God, who had guided them over the trackless sea. But to-day Germany sends her hungry, and other lands, learning the art of Bismarck in solving the problem of poverty, are transferring their poor, with the idea that here liberty means license. A friend of mine, writing from New York, says: "Again and again have I seen hundreds of people swarm out of ships from Hamburg, Liverpool, Dublin and other ports, without food or shelter, without money to buy a meal of victuals or a night's lodging. I have seen them taken directly from the ship to the almshouse." Such persons do not understand our institutions and cannot appreciate them. They do not know our laws, and are therefore unable to intelligently observe them, but are here to practice their devices, in view of gratifying their own passions and appetites. Let me say once and with emphasis, that all who come are not of this class. There are grand specimens of mankind from all shores in our midst. They have an abiding welcome to all the privileges our institutions afford, but a large percentage are here to manufacture our rum.

According to the census of 1880 there are 3,152 establishments where rum is manufactured, and $118,000,000 dollars is invested in this business; 33,689 men are employed as day laborers, and they are paid $15,000,000 annually, and the net value of their annual production is $144,000,000. Adding the money invested and the wages of the workmen, and the income, we have the enormous aggregate of $277,000,000. Of the 50,000 men employed in our distilleries as distillers, 40,000 of them are foreigners; and they are also running our saloons. Take the business directory of any of our cities, or walk the streets of Chicago, New York or Boston, and you will find very few Americans in the saloon business. If there, they are ashamed to put their signs out. Attend a saloon-keepers' convention or read in the morning papers a list of the officers. Glance over the programme for the day. Go to the hall, see who is president, who are the vice-presidents; they are nearly all foreigners. To be more accurate, take Philadelphia, that old Quaker city. There are 8,034 persons in the rum traffic, and who are they? Chinamen 2, Jews 2, Italians 18, Spaniards 140, Welsh 160, French 285, Scotch 495, English 586, Germans 2,179, Irishmen 3,041, Africans 265, Americans 205. Of this number 3,696 are females, all foreigners but one. We are bound to look this thing squarely in the face, for, as Mr. Gladstone recently said in the House of Commons, "We suffer more year by year from intemperance than from war, pestilence and famine combined, and this scourge, resulting in ruin and death, is carried on largely by foreigners."

Our second great danger, it appears to me, is that of indifference to the claims of the government. As a general proposition, every man claiming home and protection in a republic should become familiar with the laws and institutions of his home and identify himself with their supporters. Suffrage to-day means more than it ever did before. The elements to be controlled and the influences to be directed were never so potent as to-day; and yet this is no longer a government for the people or run by the people, but for the few, to be run by the few, and in this is danger. Too many stay away from the polls, caucuses and conventions, and we are too largely guided by the thoughts of a few leaders. These stay-away men are the curse of the land. They are not foreigners but Americans, who complain that their convictions are not fairly represented or expressed. In 1880 the entire foreign vote was 1,200,000, while the registered voters who failed to appear at the polls numbered 4,000,000. Where were these men to be found? Eighty thousand of them in old Ohio, sons of the Buckeye State; 280,000 in New York; 195,000 in Pennsylvania. What an army of men to fail in time of duty, and the failure to appear in the preliminary caucuses is still worse. In New York City in 1885 there were 260,000 voters; only 25,000 of whom appeared in the preliminary caucuses, leaving 235,000 men who failed to appear in the hour of New York's emergency.

In a republic like this, and in a great city like New York, where every man is a prince, and eternal vigilance is the price of liberty, certainly the voters ought to feel that the interest at the polls is paramount to all other interests on the day of the election.

The third great danger, as it appears to me, is the sectional feeling that is growing up in this country, the creating of new Swedens, Africas, Irelands, Germanys and Englands. This is all wrong. We want one people, one language, one spirit throughout the land. Mr. Thomas did us great harm, not intentionally, but really, when he went abroad to introduce a new Sweden into this country. For with this comes the secret life and plots of the nations represented, and anything that strikes against the life of our institutions, or the principles upon which they are laid, is dangerous, and cannot with safety be tolerated. We make no war upon churches or religious convictions. Every man has a right to be a Methodist, a Presbyterian or a Roman Catholic. But palsied be the hand raised to strike at, or the tongue moved to declare against, our American institutions!

We cannot tolerate sectional feeling in this country. The flag must be the emblem of liberty, equal rights and national unity to every man everywhere. "A star for every State and a State for every star." I hope the day will speedily come when no other flag can with safety be unfurled on these shores. Let the stars and stripes float on all occasions and for all interests, from sea to sea. Down in the State of Maine a very ignorant backwoodsman, having rendered some service to the Governor, was sent a com-

mission as justice of the peace. He took it out of
the post-office, looked it over, and, being unable to
read it, became alarmed. He thought it a warrant
against him for some crime, but was soon told that
it was a commission. "What am I to do with it?"
said he. "Why, you are to solemnize marriages,
and in time of a riot you are to say, "In the name
of the State of Maine I command order, and that
you disperse to your homes." Not long after, this
justice of the peace was in the city of New York,
and, walking down Broadway, he encountered an
immense mob. He at once thought of his commission, and, stepping upon the curbstone, cried out:
"In the name of the State of Maine, I command
order, and that you disperse to your homes." In
less than a minute he was knocked senseless and
carried to the lockup. On being brought before the
court he answered that he was a justice of the peace
down in Maine, and produced his papers. A laugh
went around the court room, and then the judge explained that he had no prerogative or rights outside
the State of Maine. On returning to his home a
couple waited upon him to be married. He married
them, and, after pronouncing them husband and
wife, he said: "Now, this is all right so long as you
live in the State of Maine, but should you ever venture outside the State, this ceremony is not binding."

Not so with the dear old flag. Its silken folds
bring the same blessings of peace and protection to
the dwellers on the rock-bound shores of old Maine

or to the sun-kissed slopes of California, as to the dwellers on the ever-green shores of Florida, and the snow-clad hills of Alaska.

It is six thousand miles from the fisheries of the Pine Tree State to the shores of our great American ice house; and every foot of these six thousand miles is represented by the stars and stripes.

"The union of lakes, the union of lands,
    The union of States none can sever;
The union of hearts, the union of hands,
    And the flag of our union for ever.

The union is river, lake, ocean and sky;
Man breaks not the medal when God cuts the die.
Though darkened with sulphur, though cloven with steel,
The blue arch will brighten, the waters will heal."

There is still hope for the republic; though evils exist, they are soon crushed. Anarchists are hanged, boodlers imprisoned, and our murderers, though their deeds be perpetrated in high-sounding institutions, must flee or swing. The safeguards of the nation are to be strengthened by perpetuating our institutions.

First: That of our homes, which measure the nation's strength more largely than any other; they are institutions of learning out of which come the nation's guards. To-day we have the largest standing army on the face of the earth, because the work is done in the homes. I do not mean the regular army; I mean the standing army made up of 60,000,000 people, ready at a moment's call to spring into line for the nation's defence.

If you would destroy the seeds of socialism and anarchy, encourage the home-building associations of this country.

For when a man has a home and owns his house, he is no longer a socialist or an anarchist. He believes in protection and law, because he wants to be protected. Philadelphia, through the Home Building Associations, has helped 50,000 men to own their homes. What is the result? They have neither strikes or boycotting.

"Man has many a passage through which he loves to roam,
But the middle aisle is sacred to the old, old home."

Let us see to it that we do our part in making home an institution for the training of Americans, by helping them to that cheer, sunshine and health that belongs to an American.

Secondly: Let us see to it that our schools are well provided for. We must not simply look after the illiteracy of our country. Our public school system, guarded and protected, will remove all illiteracy, and destroy the possibility of breeding hoodlums. I hope the day will soon come when every school shall be not only a hall of learning, but a center of patriotism, in which every boy and girl shall be so fully imbued with love of country as to become a true defender of the Constitution of the United States of America, cheerfully obedient to the laws of the land, encouraging purity and honor in public affairs, and loyally defending the flag. Then the 198,000 rooms into which are gathered daily more than

18,000,000 boys and girls will become centers of power, forbidding the possibility of insurrection or rebellion.

I know my Catholic friends do not see this in this light. We make no war upon Catholicism, but will not quietly suffer any institution, be it Catholic or pagan, to lay hands on this institution established by our fathers.

See to it that such work is done in the schools, as shall forbid the possibility of sectarian schools supplanting them.

Thirdly: The church of this country is becoming more and more the educator of patriots. In olden times it was said of a Jewish ruler: "He hath loved our nation and builded us a synagogue." The church is not an institution of any party. It is not her prerogative to become in any sense partisan, but she is to send forth statesmen, patriots. In her must center all the great forces. To-day she is the power of all others. In the great wars she has played well her part. Here the singing of songs, the offering of prayer around one common altar, is doing more to make us one, than any other exercise known to men; for sentiments woven into the spirit of melody can never be eradicated.

Who can measure the opportunity this hour sets before the young man or woman with health, culture and high ideals.

I turn to the dawn of the twentieth century. The camp-smoke of the pioneer flees before the burning rays of intelligence; dogmas no longer clog the feet of the racer, and the imaginary line no longer binds the thought of man. Then shall be builded a temple, whose dome shall shade the seas, into which shall be brought the achievements of art, science and religion, and out of which shall come an inspiration and love that in their influence shall make us more than conquerors in Him who loved us, and called us to be kings and priests unto the most high God.

"The fields are white to harvest,
  The days are speeding by;
Go forth again, ye workers,
  And work until ye die.

Yea, the night of death approaches,
  And angels in the sky
Repeat the chorus ever—
  Go, work, and *never* die."

Chaplain McCabe.

THE FLAG.

THE FLAG AS WITNESSED BY CHAPLAIN M'CABE IN LIBBY PRISON, JULY 4TH, 1863.

A company of our comrades resolved to celebrate the Fourth of July in Libby prison. Committees were appointed to perfect the arrangements. Chaplain McCabe had charge of the music. The committee on flags asked "How shall we secure a flag?" This was an all-important question, for none could celebrate without a flag. At last one suggested the possibility of making one. But where was the bunting to be obtained? One of the officers said, "I will give my nether garment." The material for stars and stripes was readily secured by others. The glorious day came but too slowly, and the Fourth was celebrated in Richmond as never before. The enthusiasm knew no bounds. The cheers and tigers at first were suppressed, but soon broke out in a thunderous applause. Their enthusiasm was so great as to arrest the attention of the guard without, and suddenly he stepped within the room. He was awed and silenced at the sight of a Union flag raised in the capital of the Rebellion by prisoners of war. In sullen silence he stepped forward, and with sacrilegious hands tore down the emblem of a nation's pride. But he could not wrench from the hearts of those poor Union prisoners what to them was the emblem of the priceless boon of heaven—love to God and native land.

CHAPTER II.

A nation is at the graves of her soldiers, in commemoration of their faithfulness.*

Coming from the busy walks of life to cemetery and field, with reverence for the heroic dead, and gratitude for the patriotic living, we bring a wreath of cypress for the graves of those whose lips are sealed—who answer no more to the roll-call among the living—and speak a word to those more fortunate, who fought a good fight, kept a sacred faith, won a glorious victory, and live to fight the battles of a free and ever-growing people.

We come to linger amid these graves, which are not simply houses for the dead, but vaults in which the nation's power, fame and glory are stored. They are still centers of power in cemetery, churchyard, lonely lawns, groves and national fields, beautified and indicated by shafts and slabs, deserted, forgotten, and covered with turf, visited for the first time for a year—visited by friends with loving hearts, and by angels, at the hand of the winds. See them coming from the hillside and valley, from hot-house and conservatory; coming with flowers—

*Oration delivered at Galva, Ill., Decoration Day, 1886.

flowers gathered, selected, cultivated; flowers, "nature's sweetest gifts" and choicest offerings.

There are newly-made graves, into which many of our most honored comrades have stepped since last we met. They were brave, gallant and peerless, but they have passed the Appomattox of life. Those who were:

> "The pillar of a people's hope,
> The center of a world's desire."

They have exchanged the corruptible for incorruption, mortality for immortality, and joined Moses and Joshua, Wellington and Cromwell, Lincoln and Garfield, and that innumerable throng, "whose death was a poem, the music of which can never be sung." Alas!

> "The boast of heraldry, the pomp of power,
> And all that beauty, all that wealth e'er gave,
> Await alike the inevitable hour;—
> The path of glory leads but to the grave."

Every heart in this broad land ought to respond to the call of our commander, and enter into the service of this hour with the same zeal and enthusiasm that characterized the days of enlistment, and the organization of the armies out of which these men have fallen.

Other lands have had heroes, but ours were more —they were saviours, and by their sacrifices have saved the greatest land under the shining sun.

If we glance at the fields upon which great battles have been fought and where great wars have been waged, we gain an idea of the immensity of our conflict. In the battles of Napoleon 6,000,000 brave men fell. In the thirty years' war of Germany 12,000,000 men bit the dust. In the war under Sesostris no less than 15,000,000 were slain. In the Justinian wars 20,000,000 men never returned to tell the story. In the Jewish wars more than 25,000,000 were slain. In the crusades led by Peter the Hermit and others, it is estimated that 80,000,000 fell. In Russian wars historians say 180,000,000 did not live through the contests in which they were engaged; and if we could see all who have fallen in battle, marshalled on this earth, they would outnumber the present population again and again. Some statisticians say if they were stood side by side, they would reach around this globe 1,788 times.

But our actual field of battle was larger than the fields upon which any of these wars were waged. It seemed as if the world trembled in the wars of Cromwell; but our field was larger than all the British Isles combined. Wellington touched upon the shores of Spain; but Spain, including the Canary Islands, is but a little more than half as large as Texas. France was a field of war; but France is but little larger than Maryland and California. In the mighty wars of Italy the world shook; but all Italy is but a trifle larger than the State of Nevada. Our blood is thrilled when we read of the wars of ancient Greece; but Greece is smaller than the State of West Virginia.

A SACRIFICE.

Our comrades were victors, so were others too soon forgotten. Russia, Prussia and England sent their millions on to victorious conquests, but they went into the service to learn the art of fighting —to be soldiers, and share the promotions and honors of war. Our boys went to conquer a rebellion and save the unity of a nation.

When Marcus Curtius was told by the soothsayer that the chasm opened in the Roman Forum must be filled with Romans most valued, he mounted his horse and rode away into death, a sacrifice for his country.

But President Lincoln said there must be offered 75,000 men, and then 100,000, and hundreds of thousands of America's best men, to fill the chasm of rebellion; and as oft as he called they answered, until 500,000 marched away unto death, a sacrifice

"For the land of the free
And the home of the brave."

Let Scott sing of "Clan Alpine," Macaulay tell of Horatius holding the bridge, and Tennyson write of the "Light Brigade"; but what Scottish chief, Roman warrior or English veteran ever sacrificed with American soldiers.

Their only desire was the death of the rebellion. When General Pemberton met his old comrade, General Grant, at Vicksburg, and asked for an interview, that bloodshed might cease, Grant's answer voiced the feelings of every true soldier: "On one condition this blood may cease to flow." "What is that?" "An unconditional surrender on your part, General." This spirit filled the ranks, as well as the officers.

A chaplain of the late war, Mr. Lyford, passing through the cars after the famous battle of the Wilderness, saw a wounded man making great ado. He had lain on the field three days and nights, unattended. Said the chaplain, "My son, many a boy would have rejoiced if he could have come out of that fight as well off as you are." "Oh, chaplain, you misapprehend me. I am not mourning over my wounds, but they say my leg must be amputated; if so, I cannot return and see the final victory."

A poor boy, dying, leaning against a tree, when one of his comrades took his canteen and wet his lips, revived to say, "Mother! Jesus!" Then, with his last strength, he pushed away the comrade, saying, "Follow the flag,"—choosing rather to die alone than have the flag trail in the dust or suffer defeat. Heroic boy! His record is on high.

John Jordan said, in reply to General Garfield's query, "I made no trade with God for life." "What do you mean?" said the General. "I mean, I will carry that message, sir." I have seen these men cut in pieces, torn in twain, die on the cold ground, and taken their last farewell, but never a murmur.

We remember them not simply because of Petersburg, Gettysburg and Richmond—not because they were soldiers, victors, brave and heroic. They were all these, and more—they were martyrs. They died for us, for the national honor that was threatened. For this they shall be honored in the far-off future; and as the boy stops in his history at Pompeii, to honor the soldiers buried in its gateway by Vesuvius' mad freak, so our children's children will stop in the gateways of Richmond, Petersburg, Vicksburg and Pittsburg Landing, and honor the stately forms of the American soldiers who fell rather than leave their posts, and as every schoolboy remembers to honor John Maynard for taking Elijah's chariot that others might stay, believing it:

> "Better, like Hector, on the field to die,
> Than, like a perfumed Paris, turn and fly."

We come to speak of American soldiers, and to cover their graves, as Moses covered the burning bush and the speaking mountain, with a history that shall inspire the prophets of state until hope is lost in the full fruition of brotherly love.

Again, we recall the lives and deeds of others, who suffered as much in staying at home, as those who went to battle.

At the close of a meeting held in the interest of the War, in Batavia, New York, a man with locks white for the grave came to the altar, and, taking the speaker by the hand, said: "My first son was slain at Vicksburg, my second was killed at Chickamauga, my third and last has just gone down at Petersburg; and now if the government wants what little property I have, it can have it; and then, if it will take the old man, it can have him; better that all should go than that the best government God ever gave to man should perish."

Such was the spirit that filled many a breast and home, which deserves mention for helping with the sacrifice made.

Again, we forget not our enemies in this service, for our fight was not for power to destroy men, but for union. True patriotism rejoices not over the death of its foe, but in the success of its principles. Many a night was spent in making the enemy's wounded and captured comfortable. All night we have watched by the wounded enemy, waiting for the coming surgeon. A scene in the life of our lamented President, whose life and death has employed so much of our thought for the last year, is given by his biographer. When Rosecrans fought the battle of Chickamauga, he decided that Thomas must be informed of the situation. Generals Garfield and Gano, and their orderlies, set out for a dash into the camp, and were met by the enemy. Both orderlies were killed; Gano was wounded and his horse killed, and Garfield's horse wounded twice. On that ride, in such an hour, he sees a hut, out of which crawls a number of Southern soldiers, sick and dying with hunger. Gen. Garfield stops and asks, "What can I do for you?"

"Don't come near, we have the small-pox; but give us some money to get bread, lest we die!"

True to the spirit of a soldier, he throws them his

wallet with its contents, and dashes away, saying, "Farewell; God bless you!"

This spirit may have prolonged the war; but 'twere better to do right and suffer, than to do wrong and find release.

Better or worse—the facts are historic and unalterable. All questions of what might have been done are settled by the lapse of time. The Chickahominy, Rappahannock, Shenandoah, James, Potomac and Mississippi are written all over and along their banks with blood, and monuments that tell what *was done;* not what might have been.

A generation has been born and bred in the South since we asked our conquered brothers to come back and share with us; a thousand interests have developed that claim our attention; and there remains but one thing for us to do, and that is well expressed in an old hymn:

> To serve the present age,
> My calling to fulfill.

Temples and institutions of learning crown our hills; while the generation born since the war, and now in the majority, needs the patriotism such an hour begets. If there were no words spoken, or songs sung; an hour among the heroic dead, with muffled tread and silent prayer, would impress us with a sense of their self-sacrifice, and inspire a heroism the age needs. None can move among the disembodied spirits of such men without profit. To go again in imagination in search of water to slake the thirst of a dying comrade; to note the tear of joy falling over his unwashed cheek, as we took his last farewell, is to put on anew the spirit of other days.

This is a service more catholic than others of similar claims. The nation turns from its busy marts to the mountains, whose ragged brows offer flowers for decorating the graves in the valley, regardless of distinctions, political or religious.

We listen alike to one common call of indebtedness, to those who fell in defence of the principles that make this a land of liberty.

And, with the spirit of the sisters of old, we cover the nation's graves with flowers too dear for other use. We come, at the call of our leaders, removed from all criticism by law, coming "with no blast of war blown in our ears, to imitate the tiger," but with peace in all our borders, prosperity in all our land; a smiling heaven above, a flowery mat beneath, and hope infinite in gifts filling our hearts. We come to praise God for all the past, and for the spirit that offered 500,000 men a living sacrifice in the hour of peril.

But let us not forget the price of liberty, nor suffer our citizens to become indifferent to its claims; for if we fail to transmit the patriotism of the fathers, this nation will drift into the regions of indulgence and doubt; and when the last scarred veteran, with empty sleeve and false limb, has gone to his grave, you will cease to recall the lessons taught by the history of the past.

A day among the graves of our honored dead, with this generation is, therefore, of untold worth to us. Silence your orators, muffle your drums; put away all regimentals, if you please, but the grave cannot be silenced. The veteran feels as he cannot feel elsewhere. He hears the bugle-call, and leaves his comrade again. He hears the cry of the wounded, and takes the farewell message.

This day, at Antietam, Gettysburg, Vicksburg, Petersburg and Richmond, thousands recall the conflicts of the Rebellion; and every throb of the heart is creative of that patriotism so essential to the preservation and well-being of a free government. Thus our homes are made better, and home interests become dearer than life itself. What would the Ethiopian do in his sandy desert but for his devotion, arising from the fact that a service teaches him that God made his home, and entrusted angels with the forming of all the rest of the earth?

The Norwegians, proud of their barren summits, write upon their currency, "Spirit, Loyalty, Valor;" and whatever is honorable, let the world learn it among the rocks of Norway.

The sight of these regimentals, flags and graves translates us to the day of sacrifice; and as we climb the rugged mountain for flowers, and the higher mountains of thought, our love burns for this our beloved land.

God grant that the spirit of '76 and '61 may fill the hearts of all this generation with that devotion that watched, fought and prayed the victories down upon us. Oh, may our prayers take on the spirit of Him who died in our stead; that when these organizations cease, and the last veteran sleeps, the principle of devotion to right may live and lead others, with willing hands, to bring out the flags, torn by "lead long lost," in honor of American soldiers. Then in the far-off future, some angel will sing, "They never fail, who die in a good cause;" their country glorifies their names, and memory embalms their heroic deeds.

But there are clouds to-day, that a June sun cannot burn away. A brother, whose youthful form shared my bed and mother's good-night, is sleeping in an unknown grave, visited by strangers and baptized with a stranger's tears; and this is true of many who, to-day, have not the sweet consolation of honoring their dead and decorating their graves; for they know not where they lie. Perchance old ocean's restless waves are now murmuring a requiem over their unmarked resting places. Thousands sleep on rebel soil, and

> "Sorrow and love go side by side;
> Nor height nor depth can e'er divide
>   Their heaven-appointed bands.
> Those dear associates are one;—
> Not till the race of life is run
>   Disjoin their wedded hands."

The prayers of this land will, to-day, have a new motive, touched upon by the spirits of those who will rest in unknown graves until the last trumpet of the archangel shall arouse the sleeping dead.

But this service should not end in selfishness. The spirit is too catholic and divine. We owe it to others; to the memory of the fallen.

Out of sight, out of thought, is cruel and selfish. They suffered for us many days of weariness and pain; and shall not we spend one of three hundred and sixty-five in respect to their memory? Can we be true to our manhood and withhold such service? It is only doing unto others, as we would that they should do unto us; for there is an inherent desire in every soul to be remembered. The mounds of Mexico and the far west, the well-tombs of Peru, the memorials of Palestine and the songs of the poets, all stand out in proof of this desire.

What more cruel than to be forgotten by our friends and comrades; our names and deeds to find no mention? The mariner flings his farewell kiss, with a "Remember me." The soldier wrote in his blood, "Remember me." And we all say:

> ' Death shall not claim the immortal mind;
> Let earth close o'er its sacred trust,
> Yet goodness dies not in the dust."

Our divine Lord silenced the murmuring throng at His anointing, with words of commendation co-extensive with the gospel He preached.

Rising higher, and entering the secret chamber of His own soul, we find him framing a memorial service, to perpetuate His own memory throughout all time: "This do in remembrance of me."

In this He voiced the chorus of nature:

> "There seems a voice in every gale,
>   A tongue in every flower,
> Which tells, O Lord, the wondrous tale
>   Of Thy Almighty power.
>
> The birds that rise on quivering wing
>   Proclaim their Maker's praise;
> And all the mingling sounds of spring
>   To Thee an anthem raise.
>
> Shall I be mute, Great God, alone,
>   'Midst nature's loud acclaim?
> Shall not my heart, with answering tone,
>   Breathe forth Thy holy name?
>
> All nature's debt is small, to mine;
>   Nature shall cease to be;
> Thou gavest proof of love divine—
>   Immortal life to me."

In view of this law of desire, history has been, and is being, written. For this, the halls and galleries are filled with familiar faces and forms.

And in obedience to this claim we come here, with music and flowers, to say to our comrades, "We remember thee. Thou shalt never be forgotten."

The names of George Washington, Abraham Lincoln, the anniversary of Independence and Decoration Day, will never disappear from American history

Though the old blood-stained roll will waste, this service will perpetuate itself so long as the principles for which our comrades died are cherished.

This organization will soon be gone. Every form, once clothed in blue, will have passed from our sight; and no children of soldiers can close the wasted ranks; no bread-box nor marble slab will then mark the graves of soldiers. Gettysburg and Arlington will be alive to other interests; while angels look in vain for forms, and cease to whisper, "He was loved." But the service will live when these cheeks are pale in ashes; memorial days will be brighter and American soldiers more honored. They will be respected more and more, as the future unrolls itself. He who said, "Remember Me," will never cease to scatter flowers over the sacred dead; and this nation will never get so busy as to forget its martyrs. The scarlet shroud, and the torn flag will live while history publishes its secrets; and when the questions are settled, and on the principles "for which they fell," a temple shall be builded for liberty, justice and religion, whose dome shall overshadow the land from the Pacific to the Atlantic; and hundreds of millions gather here with fruits of industry, art, science, learning and religion. Then universal freedom shall honor the founders and saviours of this land by remembering their graves.

We have reached the day of greater conquests on broader fields, with more subtle enemies.

When the war closed, all were so tired of its ways that they were ready to do almost anything for peace, and mistakes were made; everybody seemed touched by our angel of peace.

The victors pitied their enemies; and, with a magnanimity that appears nowhere else in history, we said, "Brothers, come back and share alike with us, and let us be friends, and try again."

But the friends of a lost cause were in a different attitude; and when they had rallied from their shock, they appropriated the offer to make it the cause of another battle; and to-day they are gaining in the halls and at the ballot-box, what they lost in the war.

The leaders talk of a lost cause, but cherish the same spirit. They honor the most prominent rebel of the country as a returning conqueror; while he, with the flippancy of a modern infidel, tells the world that the rebellion of '61 was for a righteous cause, and we are called upon to pay equal honors to the boys in blue and those in gray.

Shall this open the eyes of the North? If not, what will? Gentlemen, we have a work yet in this country; and the boys who fought in blue must stand together, and by their friends, until peace reigns and men love peace in righteousness.

Would it not have been better for North and South to have held the conquered territory under discipline for ten or fifteen years, and given them to feel some responsibility, before they came back to the rights of citizenship? Yes; but that day has gone by.

We are this side of a civil war, and the partisans are scattered and dying. Twenty years more will dissolve associations, and leave only here and there a lonely soldier.

Then let us grapple the priceless commodities left us; and remember that to have lived in the nineteenth century in America, will be an awful account to meet in the roll-call of eternity.

With 60,000,000 free spirits to be educated in republican and New Testament ideas, so that they may govern themselves and abide in safety, will require statesmanship of the highest character.

The machinery for subduing the wild prairies and forests, employing the tides, controlling the energies, marshalling the wealth, distributing the revenue, is vast and complete; but how to utilize it is yet a matter of study.

To educate the 2,000,000 persons now in our midst, unable to read their ballot, and yet holding the balance of power—who control thirty-two senatorial seats and 138 electoral votes, that can at any presidential election change the life of more than 200,000 employes, ought to call us to action. The turning of the rum and tobacco interests and forces, now representing $1,474,000,000 of wealth from the channel of sorrow, waste and death into the channels of enterprise and prosperity, by the opening of the gates of the whole world to our manufacturing interests, is also very important.

The mingling of nationalities in political freedom is upon us. How shall we make the African, Italian, German, Irishman, Frenchman, Indian and Norwegian into Americans; and so assimilate their peculiarities into the body politic, as to strengthen our republican institutions, is a momentous question. Now they are factors for party quarrels, and are bought by politicians, in seeking for the promotion of selfish interests.

When I recall that in 1880 there were 6,679,943 persons of foreign birth in our land, representing twenty-two kingdoms and forms of government; almost 2,000,000 from Ireland, bringing that jealousy arising from their peculiar relation to Scotland and England; and nearly 3,300,000 unable to speak our language, and utterly ignorant of Anglo-Saxon rules; and when I remember that no other nation or kingdom on which the sun shines confers citizenship so recklessly, and the fact that we are growing more lax to duty, I shudder.

In 1844 a judge was tried and removed from office in Louisiana for issuing 400 certificates of naturalization in one day, claiming to have examined 800 voters as to their age, character and residence in that time. For this, Judge Elliot was removed from office. Twenty years later, in New York, one judge made in one day 800 voters; and in 1869, 8,468 certificates were issued, and ten witnesses testified to the age, character and residence of all; one man claiming to know, personally, 2,162 worthy of citizenship; and neither of these parties was impeached. "Thus bad begins, and worse remains behind."

This mighty tide of immigration now used by

politicians for party purposes, and often in a way that leaves the material like old iron, worthless to society until melted down and recast, must be met by Christians, who will mould them into princes; for truth and righteousness, liberty and truth, must prevail. An eminent countryman of ours once said: "Stop the march of liberty?" As well might the boys of Boston mount the State House steeple some lustrous night, and call on the stars to stop in their courses. Gently, but irresistibly, the greater and lesser bear move around the pole; Orion, with his mighty trail, comes up the sky, and the Bull, the Heavenly Twins, the Crab, the Lion, the Maid, the Scales, and all that shining company pursue their heavenly march night and day. The urchins in their lofty places grow tired, sleepy and ashamed, while liberty moves steadily onward.

So live, my comrades, that you may increase the honor of those of whom the poet sings:

> On fame's eternal camping-ground
>   Their silent tents have spread,
> While glory guards with solemn round,
>   The bivouac of the dead.

For those no death bed's lingering shade;
  At Honor's trumpet call,
With knitted brow and lifted blade,
  In Glory's arms they fall.
—Holmes.

  Upon a nations grateful heart,
    They're written down by memory's pen;
  And time shall never dare erase
    The deeds of patriotic men.
Barker.

Let holy tears bedew the graves
  Of those who fell in fight;
Let marble stones above their bones,
  Salute the morning light;
Let History write in golden books;
  Let bards with song enshrine;
Let women chant the name of Grant,
  And the glory of the Line!
—Everhart.

  Gashed with honorable scars,
    Low in Glory's lap they lie;
  Though they fell, they fell like stars
    Streaming splendor through the sky.
—Montgomery

U. S. GRANT

When the stars shall wane out from the sky
Then the name of a Grant shall die.
—*Barker.*

Above all Greek, above all Roman fame.
—*Pope.*

Unbounded courage and compassion joined,
Tempering each other in the victor's mind,
Alternately proclaim him good and great,
And make the hero and the man complete.
—*Addison.*

Another veteran sinks to rest;
　His earthly pilgrimage is o'er,
His last dread battle now is fought,
　And he has made a happier shore.

When recollection leaves her throne,
　When liberty and life are not,
When ancient chaos holds its reign,
　Then veterans shall be forgot.
—*Barker.*

How shall we rank thee upon glory's page?
Thou more than soldier, and just less than sage.
—*Moore.*

(LIV.)

Gen. U. S. GRANT.

CHAPTER III.

SERMON PREACHED AT MARTHA'S VINEYARD, AUGUST 2, 1885.*

"Even so must the Son of Man be lifted up." This is one of the few scenes of Old Testament record used by our Lord, in unfolding His system of salvation. Its age gives it strength and character; for time clothes events and characters of value with power to command the attention of thoughtful men, as no other ordeal can.

We stand in the presence of an old tree, through whose branches the winds of a century have swept, as in the presence of a historian. It has the secrets of a century. Birds and beasts have found a shelter in and beneath its branches. It speaks of God in every fibre; and every leaf is a leaf in God's volume. Yes; age adds value. So in the works of men, wrought in keeping with right—age adds to their value. Those grand old works of the masters, whose fingers have long since found rest in the earth, are becoming more and more valuable. Each year adds to their worth.

By the same law, this picture becomes valuable to

*Sermon on the death of Grant, preached at Martha's Vineyard, August 2, 1885.

the teachers of to-day: Wrought in the studio of Moab, while Israel was on a march through the wilderness, it passed through the prophetic fires—suffered the criticism of the poetic and philosophic ages, until the coming of the Son of Man, who employed it without revision or comment, to confound a Jewish rabbi.

So the event of the past week, closing forever the earthly career of our peerless conqueror, becomes more and more a matter of interest and study for the student of military achievement and national strength; for "None but himself can be his parallel."

Twenty-nine years ago our great, heroic chieftain was unknown, even to the Governor of his own State, who said to Mr. Washburn, "Illinois has money enough, and men enough, but no one man of skill and military genius sufficient to organize and drill her soldiers."

"Call Capt. Grant, of Galena."

"Capt. Grant?" said Gov. Yates; "Who is Capt. Grant?"

Thus our dead hero waited to be lifted up, and brought to notice before the world, that men might see him, and know of his power.

None can, by searching, find out man, until circumstances of sufficient importance lead him to disclose the secrets of his own power.

Grant was not a creator of circumstances; had not opportunities sought him, the world would have been ignorant of the gifts God stored in him.

Like the gold stored in the hills, he lacked the ability to disclose himself.

No one could have suspected the designs of Providence, in selecting him to be sent to West Point.

But when the opportunity presented itself, he became mightier than Hercules, who crushed the two serpents sent to destroy him in his cradle; for he conquered himself and the reputation his dark days brought to him, and was ordained with the ointment of war.

Entering the storm, almost unknown, he eagerly sought for such fields as Donelson, Shiloh, Vicksburg, Chickamauga, The Wilderness, Spottsylvania, Petersburg and Appomattox; and ever after was known as the hero of Appomattox.

Thus in four years a man, comparatively unknown, has come to be one of the best known men in the world, by being lifted up.

In keeping with this, we find that certain principles, after sleeping for ages, undisturbed, in the pathway of nations, have suddenly developed into factors in the world's progress.

History is replete with illustrations of this fact. Take the mission of electricity, which was a matter of discourse as early as 600 years B. C.; and yet it slept undeveloped and undisturbed in the pathway of man for centuries, waiting for some brain with force enough to lift it. The world waited for the voice that now speaks; but waited in silence, employing birds, horses and steam to carry news. Not until the sixteenth century did men know of its power; and only in the nineteenth did man lift it up, and turn the attention of the race towards its wonders. No; it must wait until Morse could persuade an American Congress to try the experiment. He, with convictions all-controlling, conquered the indifference of that whole body, and led them to action. Yet in all the centuries electricity was the same—the free gift of God to man—waiting to speak and burn, when once intelligently employed. This principle holds good in all conditions of life known to man; it holds true concerning the Man Jesus, promised in the seed of woman. He waited in the pathway of the race, with blessings all divine, while suffering millions went mourning down to death, ignorant of the Christ; and yet every man, woman and child, when born of God, and initiated into His service, expects to reveal Him at once so that every hearer shall accept Him.

He must be lifted into power. This is a matter of vast importance; for most men make gods like unto themselves; and, knowing their own weakness, they stumble at the power of God. Now I suppose General Grant was as willing to crush out the rebellion when Governor Yates first commissioned him as when before Vicksburg, or Richmond, or when he marched down upon Lee in 1865; but he had not the power given him at the hands of the authorities, and the confidence of the people. His power was not simply in his commission. Had he been commissioned commander-in-chief in the first place, the people would have looked on him as inexperienced; and watched his undertaking with grave doubts. But, having filled each successive position in a way that gained and held the confidence of the people, when he took the position and called for troops, they were forthcoming without question; and had the rebellion lasted, men would have continued to have confidence in his ability.

He cannot be hidden; his name is heard everywhere. He left the war fitted for the Presidency; and the presidential office, after two terms, to receive honor at the hands of kings and princes of the earth; but nothing in all his career gave him a stronger hold upon the civilized world, than his last conflict with death; for in that he had only one purpose—holding the grim monster at bay until he should complete his memoirs, and thus place his family beyond the reach of want.

In this he illustrates the life of our divine Lord, who had all the willingness needed in saving this world; He had all the power, in that He was God, and was Son of the King of power, and Prince of peace; but it became Him in bringing many sons to glory to be made perfect through suffering—a Saviour, though slain in the purpose of God before the foundation of the world. He must ascend the staircase of miracles from Cana to Bethany, in order that He might be made perfect in His Saviourhood. He must stand amid the Jews at the grave, and exhort and speak of life; climb the mountain, that the world might hear from heaven God's approval and commission. Peter, James and John heard the voice in the clouds, saying, "This is My beloved Son, in whom I am well pleased; hear ye Him." He must walk upon the sea, travel the dark cypress and enter the grave, in order to turn its key and take death, hell and the grave with Him in His flight to glory.

It was this that gave his words abiding power—that will cause them to be remembered in the wasting firmament, when Plato's definitions shall be forgotten. This will lift Him above all those philosophers who spoke, to court criticism. He said *must* and *shall*, with no corrections in the second edition. Of this Nazarene it is written: "He spake as one having authority."

This question of power may not appear to you in its full significance; you may never have felt your utter inability to fill a given position.

I shall never forget an attempt to carry from the battle-field a comrade whose limbs were shattered; throwing his arms about my neck and baptizing me with his blood, I started; but after having carried him a short distance, found it impossible for both to escape. The missiles of death flew thick about us; when he kissed my unwashed cheek, whispered his farewells for mother, and then said, "Sergeant, you cannot carry me; we shall both be taken; lay me down, and you escape; you are willing—you would if you could; but you have not the strength." Oh, how I longed for the necessary power to do as I desired for my dying comrade. Then, for the first time in my life, did I realize my weakness. No one can ever tell what the constant effort and unceasing anxiety of the late General Grant was during the year 1863-4; watched by scheming politicians and jealous subordinates, and filled with a sense of responsibility such as his conception of national unity and sense of right must have given him. It was not to conquer the enemy and enslave them, but to bring about a condition of peace, such as would establish confidence north and south, east and west, and thereby maintain the glory of the nation.

The strength of a nation is in its power to maintain the confidence of its people under all circumstances.

Let me give you an illustration, which is neither new nor original:

In the Persian form of government there were peculiarities, such as made it impossible for a king to revoke a decree. It must remain unaltered through all time.

This is the perfection of law; and could it have been enacted in perfect wisdom, would have secured safety and security to the Persians under the reign of a perfect king. But neither perfect wisdom nor perfect manhood was found in the law-makers, or the executive powers. The king, moved by a company of jealous men, made a decree that none should offer prayer to any save himself, not knowing on whom it was to fall; and Daniel, his friend, whom the king loved, was made the subject of restraint. Daniel called upon his God, and thereby became the subject of punishment. Though the king loved him, and labored until the going down of the sun, he could not save him, and keep the law unto the maintenance of confidence in the kingdom. Nothing short of that power which controls the laws governing the fires, and holds the beasts in subjection, could save Daniel. The king must throw him into the den of lions, and thereby keep the law. But God could, and did, save him, carrying him safely through the den of lions without injury to the lions, for he belonged to another kingdom, and the lions were reserved for the next victim. So God's laws are irrevocable; made in view of the eternal security of the just and obedient. A violation of any one of these laws, passed unnoticed, would compromise the whole system of God's government. Among the many laws of God is found this: "The soul that sinneth, it shall die." That law must be kept; the honor must be preserved, or confidence in all the code is compromised. Sinners must be thrown under the law of death; the purity and sanctity of heaven is in question.

General Grant was unselfish in his devotion and loyalty to America, his native land. He inherited a Puritanic faith; and, as the Rev. Dr. Fawcett, of Aurora, Ill., has well said, "He was a Christian, as well as a patriot. To a company of young men who called upon him at his home in Galena, just before their starting for Europe, he said:

'Gentlemen, never forget that you are citizens of these United States, and be as careful of the good name of your country as you would be of your home.'

Truly, from this hour, with these words and memories, we will love our country more.

General Grant was a Christian. He possessed that broad, philanthropic spirit, and that unselfish generosity of soul, that is born of a Christian faith; and that ungrudgingly contributes its meed of merit to high and low, rich and poor, conspicuous and obscure. After the fall of Fort Donelson, when the soldiers, in an exuberance of delight, were glorying over the accomplished victory, General Grant sat quietly and unmoved in the midst of their shouts, and after a little he quietly raised his head and said: 'Comrades, we must not forget that it is God who gives us victory.' Standing high above envy or jealousy, having no personal purposes to serve, but only a desire to do his duty before God and his country, he contributes with the most liberal generosity to the merit of the generals, great and small, who assisted in the restoration of the Union. On that memorable Fourth of July, after the fall of Vicksburg, when dispatches of congratulation were reaching him from all great men and all cities of the North, and when his subordinates were casting their praises at his feet, he looked coolly around upon his adulators and said: 'Let us not forget the brave soldiers who have done the watching and the fighting. The glory belongs to them.' Thus, ever and always unmindful of himself, with Christian spirit he gave praise to others. It was this spirit that prompted him on the day when General Lee stood before him and offered him his sword—a token of surrender. General Grant said: 'General Lee, keep that sword; you have won it by your gallantry.' And when at the hour the Union soldiers were wont to show signs of rejoicing over the glorious victory and the return of peace, the great-hearted, the warm-hearted, Christian-hearted Grant requested that they abstain from all expressions of joy, saying: 'These are our countrymen and our brothers again.' No pomp, no show, no parade, but a broad Christian manhood, doing unto others as he would they should do unto him.

General Grant possessed a clear intellectual conception of the benefits of Christianity to his own country, and freely stated them. At the time of the marriage of his daughter, in a conversation with Bishop Simpson and others, he said, pointing to the Bible that lay before him: 'It is the Bible that makes sacred and pure the homes of our people.' In a conversation with him after his return from 'around the world,' I asked him of the mission fields of the Methodist Episcopal Church in China. He gave me a full description of three of our missions in that country, and then added: 'In China I learned to appreciate what Christianity has done for my own country.' General Grant had such a faith in Jesus as the Saviour and Comforter of men, that he went to Him in prayer in the hour of his sorrow. In a conversation with Bishop Gilbert Haven he said, in speaking of his early departure from home: 'My mother taught me when a child to go to God with my sins every night, and I have never forgotten it.' Edward D. Mansfield, in his life of the General, says: 'His earliest training was by a Christian mother, and the influence of that training is seen every day.' When in his tour around the world, he reached Jerusalem, his friends proposed to give him a grand *fete*. 'No,' said the hero, 'no ovation to me in the place where my Saviour was crucified.'

General Grant had a Christian faith that led him to hope and pray for a resting-place in heaven. The other day a devoted priest of the Roman Catholic Church visited him and told him that all the Christian people were praying for him. The general answered: 'I feel grateful to the Christian people of the land for their prayers on my behalf. This applies to all. I am a great sufferer all the time, but the facts I have related are compensation for much of it. All that I can do is to pray that the prayers of all these good people may be answered so far as to have us all meet in another and better world.' General Grant had a Christian faith that enabled him to patiently endure suffering and calmly face the realities of eternity. He has not conversed much through these months of suffering, for, like Moses, he was a man slow of speech. Doubtless his faithful and honest pastor, Dr. Newman, will have treasured away many a rich and comforting word that has not yet reached the public ear. But through all the days the eye of a nation has been turned to Mount McGregor, and there they have seen an example of uncomplaining heroism higher and better than any the history of the war contains. Vicksburg was a great victory; Lookout Mountain was a great victory; Appomattox was a great victory, but through these weeks of quiet suffering the nation has seen how much greater than the achievements of fields of battle are the household virtues and simple family affections which all men have within their reach. They have seen how the Christian lessons at a mother's knee could arm for greater war and greater victory than West Point or years on the tented field. 'Go up the mountain and die, and be gathered to thy people,' said God to Moses, and now more than a month has passed away since a like message fell upon the ear of the leader of the armies of Columbia, and he slowly, before our eyes, passed up Mount McGregor to die and be gathered to his people. Let us for a moment ascend the mountain, and stand by the bed of the departing hero. It is Wednesday evening, July 22, 1885. The sun has gone down to his rest over the western mountains, and the evening is cool and bright, and all is hushed and quiet about the mountain home, except the twitter of the birds in the lonely pines. The family are gathered at the sick man's side, and the sorrowing wife requests Dr. Newman to offer prayer. While the prayer is being offered strong men bow their heads, and tears flow down the cheeks of all. 'Now lay me down to die,' said the quiet man, and his request was heard. All night long doth love its faithful vigils keep. It is Thursday morning, July 23, 1885, at 7.04 o'clock. But hush, what is this we hear? Ah! The leader and commander has been gathered to his own people, and that which has broken the stillness of the morning is the voice of weeping over all the land. From the heart of New England, from whose loins his fathers came, we hear the voice of weeping; from his own native State we hear the voice of weeping; from Illinois, his adopted State, we hear the voice of weeping; from the far-away South comes the voice of mourning; from over the mountains comes the voice of mourning. That throb which you hear is from over the sea, for England stands with bowed head. From the fisherman's hut at the seaside, from the frontierman's cabin in the far west, we hear the voice of weeping. Under the arches of the great cathedral, and through the open windows of the humble western church, one requiem of music floats upon the morning air—'The minor strains of sorrow, for a soldier is dead.' Grant, the general; Grant, the faithful citizen; Grant, the trusting

Christian, has been gathered unto his people, while the soldiers of Columbia, in weeping columns, march to the beat of muffled drum. The heart of a great nation would give the ashes of their leader a resting place in some new Westminster at Washington, where pilgrims might visit his tomb for ever. 'And die in the mount whither thou goest up, and be gathered unto thy people.' Standing on the summit of Mount McGregor I look up, and, following the path of light until it reaches the gate of the heavenly city, I look within, and there, amid the exulting freedmen of all countries and all climes, I see Columbia's three worthies—Washington, Lincoln and Grant."

So our unconquerable hero has gone forward, until at last he has been called to mingle in the Court of the Most High, and when the roll has been called for the last time, when the last reveille has been sounded, when the last battle has been fought, the honored name of Ulysses S. Grant will be found on the unchanging pages of history as one whom God raised up for a special work; and history will show how nobly was that work done, how fearlessly were our armies led to victory by the greatest military leader of modern times. A leader who battled not for the advancement of his own interests—not that he might be at the head of an empire, but prompted by his love of right, he fought that the millions in bondage should be slaves no more, and for the triumph of right and the preservation of the Union.

Gen. JOHN A. LOGAN.

JOHN A. LOGAN

He lives on just the same as before;
This is only the blouse that he wore.
—*Barker*.

Life that dares send
A challenge to his end,
And when it comes, say, "Welcome, friend!
—*Crashaw*.

When all the blandishments of life are gone,
The coward sneaks to death the brave live on.
—*Sewell*.

Thy purpose firm is equal to the deed;
Who does the best his circumstance allows,
Does well, acts nobly; angels could do no more.
—*Young*.

He most lives
Who thinks most, feels the noblest, acts the best.
—*Bailey*.

Statesman, yet friend to truth! of soul sincere;
In action faithful, and in honor dear;
Who broke no promise, served no private end,
Who gained no title, and who lost no friend.
—*Pope*

(LXXII.)

CHAPTER IV.

ADDRESS—JOHN A. LOGAN.*

"And Hezekiah slept with his fathers, and they buried him in the chiefest of the sepulchres of the sons of David; and all Judea and the inhabitants of Jerusalem did him honor at his death."

A celebrated Russian once said: "Cursed is the nation that has no great men to govern its affairs." Another, commenting on this saying, said: "A republic needs *good* men more than she needs *great men*.

To-day our republic turns from the grave of one of her great *and* good men. Our Hezekiah is dead, and his body is laid in the sepulchre, while the nation honors him.

General John A. Logan was a great man. He was a unique, self-made American. Wherever he appears—in home, lodge, post, caucus, convention, camp, battle-field, legislative hall or church, he was John A. Logan, with no attempt to be other than himself; and, as it is written of Hezekiah of old, so will it be chronicled of Logan: "Whatsoever he began to do, he did it with his might, and prospered."

His death leaves a vacancy, never to be filled. The nation will go on, and all her interests will be

---

*Address—'John A. Logan,"—delivered Sunday morning, December 27, 1886.

cared for, for God is at the helm, and this people, many of whom loved him more than they can love any man now living, love the land he loved and the cause he fought for more than all, and will arise from this sorrow to do as he did.

It seems fitting that meetings should be held in all parts of this great land, and that honor should be given him at his death. He belonged to the nation; and it is truly fitting that we who live in Chicago, where his name is a household word, where his presence was always occasion for happy greetings, where his name appears on the records of God's militant church, and where it is hoped his dust will be interred, should speak of his achievements; note his virtues, and mourn his loss.

As a man, he was generous even to a fault. I think it would have been a virtue had he been more chary of his gifts, his services and sacrifices. We speak of his honorable poverty as though it were to be courted and cited for young men to emulate. I cannot look upon it in this light. I glory as much as any man in this nation in the integrity which kept his hands clean and his character pure; but do we want to brand every man who by prudence, forethought and industry has secured a fortune, with dishonesty and impurity?

Nay, nay; nor would our honored dead approve of this way of putting things. It was his great heart that gave, when prudence would have dictated otherwise.

In ten thousand homes to-day they will take down

a familiar picture and look through their tears at the man who shared with them because of their fellow feelings as soldiers. How many widows and orphans in this land to-day are the recipients of help from the government because John A. Logan was their friend? They paid the petty lawyer; but who thought of paying him, or when did he think of taking aught from their pittance? This characteristic of his nature opened the way for innumerable demands upon his time and energy, that must have hastened his flight and cut short his work. I heard a letter read from his pen within a week, dated December 6. Everybody claims the attention of great men; and they forget how many are making demands on one man; and sometimes we feel slighted because they do not give us more time, money and attention. Friends, remember, in a republic where all positions are secured by the patronage of the people, no public man can give any one person his undivided attention, and we are working our great men to death—robbing them of their home comforts, their means, their strength and their friends, and the nation of their lives.

He was full of sympathy. His great nature was touched and moved at the sight of suffering. This gave him a place in the hearts of the million soldiers and their families, now living, that no other man has, or can secure. If you have watched the telegrams made public since his death, you will approve of this statement.

He was a man of conviction. He did what he believed to be right, for the sake of right. He was a Democrat at the commencement of the war. He favored and supported Douglas, and did his best to elect him; but when Lincoln was declared elected, and the disloyalty of the South began to show itself, his voice was heard in Congress in defence of the Union and the support of Lincoln; and at the defeat of our troops at Bull Run, Logan's heart was stirred to its very depths. His convictions were at white heat, as his speeches show, and the thousands enlisted by him during the succeeding sixty days clearly indicate.

His convictions of right were so strong that no temptation was sufficient to sway him from the path of integrity. In 1880 he believed that Grant ought to be nominated for the third term; and many think he might have secured the nomination for himself at that time, but for his fidelity to his old commander and his unwillingness to give up the fight. This gave him the confidence of thoughtful men, and their tribute of praise is heard to-day.

General Grant said: "At the first outbreak of the war some of the people of Illinois joined the southern army; many others were preparing to do so; others rode over the country at night, denouncing the Union, and made it as necessary to guard railroad bridges over which national troops had to pass in southern Illinois as it was in Kentucky, or any of the border slave states. Logan's popularity in this district was unbounded. He knew almost enough of the people in it by their Christian names to form an ordinary congressional district. As he went in politics, so his district was sure to go. The Republican papers had been demanding to know where he stood on the questions which at that time engrossed the whole of public thought. Some were very bitter in denunciation of his silence. Logan was not a man to be coerced into an utterance by threats. He did, however, come out in a speech before the adjournment of the special session of Congress, which was convened by the President, soon after his inauguration, and announced his undying loyalty and devotion to the Union. But I had not happened to see that speech, so that when I first met Logan my impressions were those formed from reading denunciations of him. McClernand, on the other hand, had early taken strong grounds for the maintenance of the Union, and had been praised accordingly by the Republican papers. The gentlemen who presented these two members of Congress asked me if I would have any objection to their addressing my regiment. I hesitated a little before answering. It was but a few days before the time set for mustering into United States service such of the men as were willing to volunteer for three years of war. I had some doubt as to the effect a speech from Logan might have; but, as he was with McClernand, whose sentiments on the all-absorbing questions of the day were well known, I gave my consent. McClernand spoke first, and Logan followed in a speech which he has hardly equalled since for force and eloquence. He breathed a loyalty and devotion to the Union which inspired my men to such a point that they would have volunteered to remain in the army as long as an enemy of the country continued to bear arms against it. They entered the United States service almost to a man."

As a soldier, he won his greatest victories. No man was more valiant than he, none more courageous.

There seems to have been some who looked upon him with doubt when he appeared among Unionists; but his bravery, valor and fidelity during the long struggle, from '61 to '65, silenced all enemies and fixed him in the heart of the republic as "The Volunteer of the West."

He was born to be great. As a leader, he had physical courage that never failed him, and coupled with this was a moral courage that made him often unconquerable, and a will which made him the chief character among the volunteers of this country for all time; and when all else that he did or said is forgotten, his war record will be cited with pride by children's children.

In this he not only had the courage to face danger undaunted, but he made himself a leader of men by laying his plans so carefully and thoughtfully as to inspire confidence.

The army saw at a glance that their leader took in

the situation, that he worked by well-matured plans, in which he himself had such perfect confidence that they accepted the situation and followed wherever he led."

In the famous charge at Atlanta, when McPherson fell and the army halted, broke and were ready to run, Logan received orders from Sherman to assume command of the army of the Tennessee; a staff officer says, "He bowed his head and said, 'Would to God I were better qualified to fill the place he filled so perfectly.'" This inspired confidence, and putting spurs to his famous black stallion, "Old John," he rode rapidly to the line of the Seventeenth corps, where he arrived in time to save the day. When he arrived, the lines of the Sixteenth and Seventeenth were crumbling away. Dashing down the line of battle till he reached the right, Logan reined in his foaming horse with such force as to throw the animal back on his haunches. Then, riding up to a color-bearer and seizing the flag, he rode to the front and center of the line and cried: "Will you hold this line with me?" "Yes, yes!" and "Logan leads!" went up from ten thousand voices. "Then keep in line and advance. We'll whip and drive them to the sea." Each man felt that Logan in the lead was worth an army corps to fill the gap in the lines; the faltering nerved themselves for one more struggle; laggards and stragglers came from behind rocks and trees and fell into line, and, with the cry, "Logan leads!"

they hurled the rebels back, drove them into Atlanta, and, by a splendid exhibition of personal bravery and power over demoralized troops, only approached by that of Sheridan at Cedar Creek, defeat was turned into victory, and Atlanta was practically secured, with eight thousand rebel dead to attest the fierceness of the fight.

When this was over, Sherman felt obliged to appoint Howard as commander of the Army of the Tennessee, which I always regretted. Hooker resigned, but Logan returned to the Fifteenth corps, to share with his men, and on July 28th he led the famous Fifteenth in charge, and continued victorious in every fight until September 2, when Atlanta fell.

An incident is related, showing how he secured the corps badge. One day an Irishman was asked what their badge was. Smiting his cartridge-box, he said: "There is my badge, with forty rounds in it, sir." General Logan heard it, and at once adopted it as the badge for the Fifteenth corps; so from that time a cartridge-box, marked "Forty Rounds," was their corps badge.

This was characteristic of the man. He was in the war to conquer. When pressure was brought to bear on him, in 1862, to leave the army and accept the nomination for Congress, he refused, and said, "I have entered the field to die, if need be, for the government; and I never expect to return to peaceful pursuits until the object of this war has been accomplished.

A friend of his says when Logan wanted to charge upon the enemy's ranks in the Georgia campaign, McPherson ordered him to retreat, and build up fortifications and protect his men. Logan urged, protested, and did all that a subordinate could do to be allowed the privilege of fighting, and history proves that he was right. But he obeyed his superior officer, and the night following, his friend said: "I undertook to sleep with him in an ambulance, but sleep I could not, nor rest, such was the restlessness of that great soul, that, like a war-horse, he struggled all night to be free."

As a politician, he has led well, and been true to his friends and manly with his enemies. Everybody knew where to find him, and just what to expect when he was found.

He was simply a straightforward fighter for the right, as he saw it. I have not always agreed with him, but always admired his defence of positions taken, for when he had given his heaviest blows, he stood up to receive the returning blow, with a manliness commendable.

He was never malignant nor vindictive. He was a partisan; and as such, defended his party with all his power, which is commendable. The first thing for any man to do when he finds he can no longer defend the church or party of which he is a member, is to sever his connection, and find a home elsewhere. This he will do if he be an honest man, and such was our brother.

The Confederate soldiers say: "He was a warm friend, a brave enemy, and an honest man, and we lay upon his coffin the memorial, not indeed of those who loved him during his life, but of those who, in his death, recall only his virtues." Those stirring virtues were numerous and positive. Of an ardent nature, he did nothing by halves. Ambitious he was, undoubtedly, but his aspirations lay in the direction of patriotic advancement and elevation, and sought no devious routes or unmanly advantage. During an age of corruption his han's were clean, and his career shows how he stood the ordeal of a national political campaign without dishonor, coming out of the contest with an untarnished reputation, and more respected than when he entered it.

His civil service compares well with that of the best men we have been blest with. He was not a Lincoln, Sumner or Grant, but he was a student of sturdy habits. His speeches in the Senate and on the stump show him to have been a broad, earnest student of men and interests. He knew the American people, and few men created greater enthusiasm in the campaign of 1884 than our lamented comrade. Wherever he went few were ever given a better hearing or had more influence in leading men to act in harmony with their thought.

His great effort in the Fitz John Porter case was his masterpiece, showing a force of argument, illustration and eloquence that surpasses that of any year in his whole career, which is a lesson to all men in public life who are relaxing their hold, losing their influence, and retiring, because they have reached the dead-line of fifty. Here was a self-made man, in his sixty-first year, reaching his climax with a reserve force that promised better works the next time, had he lived; and occasion called.

When General Logan's death was announced to him, James G. Blaine thus briefly summarized his character: "General Logan was a man of immense force in a legislative body. His will was unbending; his courage, both moral and physical, was of the highest order. I never knew a more fearless man. He did not quail before public opinion when he had once made up his mind, any more than he did before the guns of the enemy, when he headed a charge of his enthusiastic troops.

In debate he was aggressive, and I have had occasion to say before, and I now repeat, that while there have been more illustrious military leaders in the United States, and more illustrious leaders in legislative halls, there has been no man, I think, in this country, who has combined the two careers in so eminent a degree as General Logan."

He was a Christian. When we have said all that could be said for him as a man, husband, father, friend, soldier, politician and statesman, we must admit that he was more than all these, for these were but the results. He was a Christian. Said Dr. Edwards, who knew him well: "He claimed not to be a model in personal consecration, or in the profounder experiences of the spiritual life, but we believe him to be a modest, honest, unpretentious Christian citizen. Political competitions are cruelly unsparing, and General Logan's very church relations have been subjects of criticism among men who would have made a political trade with Judas, if the latter had but promised his casting vote. From our own professional and personal standpoint in our church, we have seen that which compelled faith in the Christian sincerity and unquestionable genuineness of John A. Logan. In the ardor of public movement and the earnestness of pressing issues, we have sometimes differed from him, but never in anything that for an instant impeached his character, or governing motive."

His pastor and friend, Dr. F. M. Bristol, says: "No man ever more devotedly cherished the principles and admired the character of Christ than General Logan; but no Christian was ever more sincerely modest in assuming that name. He could not be a hypocrite in religion any more than in politics. He never spoke lightly on sacred themes, nor made a jest of other men's honest convictions, whether they agreed with his own or not. He was liberal and high-minded enough to grant to every other man the same right of independent opinion which he claimed and exercised for himself. He made no profession of saintliness; but he made proof of his manliness. From the mortal, human side, home was his religion, duty his creed; his country was his altar, his sacrifice his own blood, and his record was glory and a nation's gratitude."

For more than fifteen years General Logan was a member of the Methodist Episcopal Church, and a greater portion of that time was connected with Trinity Church, of Chicago, where he was ever heartily welcomed by a people who loved and admired him and his. His several pastors often had the privilege of administering to him the holy sacrament, and of preaching in his hearing the word of God, to which he was always an attentive and sincere listener. And often has it been proved to those pastors that the death-folded hand was as tender in benevolence as it was terrific in battle. While to his praise it may be said that he never sacrificed Christian principle to political ambition, it may likewise be said to his honor that he never sacrificed a just and laudable ambition to fear, to envious criticism or to unreasonable opinions."

Bishop Newman, his pastor, said at his funeral: "Bluff, steady, honest Logan was a Christian in faith and practice. Here is his Bible, which he read with daily care. Sincere and humble, he accepted Christ as his personal Saviour. When I gave him the sacrament of the Lord's supper, too humble in spirit to kneel on the cushion around the altar, he knelt on the carpet, and, with his precious wife by his side, received the tokens of a Saviour's love. His manly brow shone like polished marble, for he felt that he was in the presence of the Searcher of all hearts.

It was his last sacrament on earth. Standing by the tomb of Grant on last Memorial Day, he delivered an oration on 'Immortality.' In that glorious hope he died. He has joined his comrades in the skies. He has answered to the morning call of eternal life."

His people's heart is his funeral urn;
   And should sculptured stone be denied him,
There will his name be found, when in turn
   We lay our heads beside him.
                              —*Smith.*

His *faith*, perhaps, in some nice tenets might
Be wrong; his *life*, I'm sure, was in the right.
                              —*Cowley.*

         Whoe'er amidst the sons
      Of reason, valor, liberty and virtue,
      Displays distinguished merit, is a noble
      Of Nature's own creating.
                              —*Thomson.*

He was not of an age, but for all time.
                              —*Tourneur.*

Emigravit is the inscription on the tombstone where he lies,
Dead he is not, but departed, for the hero never dies.
                              —*Longfellow.*

(LXXXVIII.)

GEN. PHIL. SHERIDAN.

CHAPTER V.

SHERIDAN.*

"The last words of great men embody the ruling passions of their lives. The miser, as death closes about him, clutches for his coins, the dying stage-driver reaches for his brake; the leader of men issues commands. Great-hearted Nelson, when mortally wounded, cried: 'What's the position of the enemy?' and being told, triumphantly exclaimed: 'Let me die while they are retreating.' The words of Paul to Timothy were: 'Thou, therefore, endure hardness as a good soldier of Jesus Christ.' Lying in imperial Rome, mentally comparing the victories of Cæsar and Pompey with those of Joshua and Caleb, Samuel and David, while ringing in his ears came the blows of the hammer used in constructing the block on which he was to be beheaded, he wrote these words of cheer to Timothy. Our minds have recently been drawn toward a brave soldier, the grand, heroic and gallant Phil. Sheridan, who, by identifying himself with the armies of the North, shared in the victories of the boys in blue."

His life is full of suggestions. He entered into

*Oration delivered August 12, 1888.

every service with a purpose to win, such as gave to his orders an inspiration that often became unconquerable.

To say that he was brave, seems insipid. He was more. Others as fearless have failed, and are forgotten; he added to his bravery that of heroic energy, and mental conception, such as made the most insurmountable obstacles trifling. He acted from a conviction, and not on impulse. This made him blind to difficulties, indifferent to surroundings, and alive to results.

He dashed into action with a lover's conviction of what must be done; and we follow him on to victory where others have failed. Some one has said: "He possessed a splendid tactical ability; he counted his chances; he was fertile in resource; he was quick to see the weakest point in an enemy's defence, and to turn it to his own advantage; he had a singular genius for the quick handling of his men, and for getting the best out of them; and a no less remarkable ability to extricate himself from a dangerous situation. His fertility of resource, indeed, and his ready adaptability to the unforseen emergency, often served him in good stead, and turned defeat into victory."

In olden times he would have become blood-thirsty and tyrannical; but not so in the conflict for national unity. "Alexander the Great waded through the blood of his fellow man. By the sword he conquered; and by the sword he kept the vanquished in bondage. Scarcely was he cold in death, when his vassals shook off the yoke, and his empire was dashed into fragments." But Sheridan fought to weld a nation more closely, and to put aside the question from which resulted the war; hence the humanity exhibited made our hero a man of conviction; and Sheridan represents the elements of true heroism. With courage undaunted, combined with gentleness of disposition; strong as a lion in war, gentle as a child in peace; bold, daring, fearless, undaunted, unhesitating, his courage rose with the danger; ever fertile in resources, ever prompt in execution; his rapid movements were never impelled by a blind impulse, but were prompted by a calculating mind. I have neither the time nor the ability to dwell upon his military career from the time he left West Point till the close of the war.

Let me select one incident where he reveals to us his quickness of conception and readiness of execution. I refer to his famous ride in the valley of Virginia. As he is advancing along the road, he sees his routed army rushing pell-mell toward him. Quick as thought, by the glance of his eye, by the power of his sword, by the strength of his will, he hurls back that living stream on the enemy, and snatches victory from the jaws of defeat.

Said his friend and pastor: 'On some few occasions, in Washington, I had the pleasure of meeting General Sheridan socially, in private circles. I was forcibly struck by his gentle disposition, his amiable manner, his unassuming deportment, his eye beaming with good-nature, and his voice scarcely raised above a whisper. I said to myself: Is this bashful man and retiring citizen the great general of the American army? Is this the hero of so many battles?

It is true that General Sheridan has been charged with being sometimes unnecessarily severe toward the enemy. My conversation strongly impressed me with the groundlessness of a charge which could in no wise be reconciled with the abhorrence which he expressed for the atrocities of war, with his natural aversion to bloodshed, and with the hope he uttered that he would never again be obliged to draw his sword against an enemy. I am persuaded that the sentiments of humanity ever found a congenial home, a secure lodgement in the breast of General Sheridan. Those who are best acquainted with his military career unite in saying that he never needlessly sacrificed human life, and that he loved and cared for his soldiers as a father loves and cares for his children.

But we must not forget that if the departed hero was a soldier, he was, too, a citizen, and we must ask ourselves how he stands as a son, husband and father. The parent is the source of the family, the family the source of the nation. Social life is the reflex of the family life. The stream does not rise above its source. Those who were admitted into the inner circle of General Sheridan's home need not be told that it was a peaceful and happy one. He was a fond husband and an affectionate father, lovingly devoted to his wife and children. I hope I am not trespassing on the sacred privacy of domestic life when I state that the General's sickness was accelerated, if not aggravated, by a fatiguing journey which he made in order to be home in time to assist at a domestic celebration, in which one of his children was the central figure."

Thus he will go down into history with Lincoln and Grant, and always be put in contrast with McClellan and other inefficient leaders.

The author of the "Life of Lincoln," given in the "Century," said of Sheridan: "Any one reading over his letters of this first period of his military service, is struck by the fact that through him something was always accomplished. There was absence of excuse, complaint or delay; always the report of a task performed. If his means or supplies were imperfect, he found or improvised the best available substitute; if he could not execute the full requirement, he performed as much of it as was possible."

No one characteristic is in greater demand to-day than this genius to do something. Every army has its martinets, who are forever getting ready—going to do—drilling for work, but never get to doing anything until the opportunity is lost.

There are others who are so cautious and fearful, that opposing armies become to them unconquerable, and the enemy crosses over the river and is gone, before the recruits arrive. When Moses commanded

Israel to go forward, the line was in motion before the waters moved one iota. Oh, that the spirit of doing something might come on us to-day.

Sheridan was always at work; every day made a record he could look on with pride. A celebrated artist once was found weeping at eventide, and asked why he lamented. "Ah," said he, "I have not finished one thing worthy of a place in a gallery to-day." Sheridan was always a soldier. Everybody knew he was a soldier, whether on duty, or in camp.

"He's a soldier; I know he's been a soldier, by his walk."

These words attracted my attention, as I sat in the depot, awaiting the arrival of a train. They were used in reference to an erect, firm-treading man, who had alighted from a train, and had evidently been an object of interest to his fellow passengers.

"Aye, and he's a soldier; I know by the way he carries his pack," said another.

"Yes, and by his politeness," observed a third. "Did you see how he touched his cap, only because you gentlemen looked at him? Most of us would have said, 'What are you staring at?'"

The train started off; the man left the station, and I followed. "Did you hear the remarks of your fellow travelers, my friend?"

He smiled, as I repeated them, and said: "Just as it should be, sir; just as it should be. A soldier in plain clothes, off duty, should be the same as when uniformed, and in command."

A true soldier ought to walk so as to be known as such everywhere.

He was never indifferent to the orders of his superiors. Whatever may have been his conception of the situation, orders were to be obeyed, not questioned. I once stood near him when the orders seemed most ridiculous; yet he sat on his horse, calmly over-looking the field, when a sharpshooter picked off his aide; as he fell, the General said: "Take him off;" and then, turning his eye back, held us for minutes by force of example. He simply said: "The commander knows why these orders are given, and the responsibility is with him, after they are executed."

I dare say Joshua's men wondered why they should be ordered to equip themselves as warriors, and march around Jericho once a day, for six days; and wondered more why they should be required to march seven times around the city on the seventh day; but they obeyed. God knew; and that was sufficient. They blew their rams' horns, and, with a mighty shout, the walls cracked and tumbled. They did it heartily. God requires heartiness in his service. How grandly Paul entered that service. His prospective wealth, and his deep-seated prejudice for the religion of his fathers were abandoned, and he carried his great learning, wide influence, family name, and personal authority into that service, and was ever after enthusiastic, loyal, and intensely hearty.

The age is in need of men who are willing to do what is in their power. If your sight is dim, do something that does not require fine sight. Our grandmothers abandoned fine needlework, and knit. If your blood is thin, and you chill by exposure, arouse yourself; run a little, and get up a glow. If you can't lift two hundred pounds, lift ten. If you are too old to go out to battle, be sure you enter into your closet, and pray for those who *do* go out to fight. If you are not able to give gold, give silver —give copper. If you cannot weep with the weeping, rejoice with the joyful. If you can't soar like an eagle, skim as the swallow.

If you can't be a Joshua, be an "armor-bearer." Never plead inability, or poverty, when God and His church put in their claims for service. I know a lady who never attends prayer meetings, or evening service—she is "not able;" but she accepts every invitation to tea, and to evening parties, that she receives. She never pleads absence from these places through indisposition. She lacks heart in the Lord's service. I know a family who buy every article of luxury and clothing they need. They go to any and all amusements they desire to. No complaints of poverty are made; but if God's cause needs money to push its enterprises, they plead poverty, and refuse to give. They lack heart.

Sheridan's life was an incentive to general loyalty,

such as will find ready acknowledgment, not only in the North, but also in the South. I know the Southern people; I know their chivalry, I know their magnanimity, their warm and affectionate nature; and I am sure that the sons of the South, and especially those who fought in the late war, will join in the national lamentation, and will lay a garland of mourning on the bier of the great general. They recognize the fact that the Nation's General is dead, and that his death is the Nation's loss. And this universal sympathy, coming from all sections of the country, irrespective of party lines, is easily accounted for, when we consider that under an overruling Providence, the war in which General Sheridan took such a conspicuous part has resulted in increased blessings to every State in our common country.

> "There's a divinity that shapes our ends,
> Rough hew them how we will."

And this is true of nations, as well as individuals. Our people are coming to see this, and encourage everything that is creative of true loyalty. In a word, there is in men a spirit that glories in true loyalty. I remember a scene after the battle of Sycamore Church, where our batallion was surrendered, and a number made a dash and escaped. A young soldier, just from the hospital, weak and wounded, there came to me, saying: "Where's my brother, Steve?" I told him I had seen him stripped of coat and shoes and marched off toward

Libby, as a prisoner. He said: "I'll take his place;" and he did, and fought bravely on. On another occasion, while McClellan was keeping us in the mud, on the Potomac, a drummer boy was shot. The bone in his leg was shattered. A battle was on. He said: "Carry me on your shoulder, and let me drum it out." Of such stuff are heroes made. Sheridan was loyal to what he believed right. Oh, for more such heroes. Do right. I'd rather go to heaven through the poor-house, than to hell through a mansion. Soldiers must be aggressive. Let Christians get this spirit, and we can take Chicago for Christ. We can crowd the churches and the chariots until God will have to enlarge his heaven, to accommodate the hosts who will come up. I have a small parchment at my home. It could be folded up in the thimble my mother wore on her finger. All the money in Chicago would not buy it —that honorable discharge from the army. I look ahead to another discharge. Not one of parchment, but a white stone, surrounded by the sanctified, who trail their white robes on the golden paving of the New Jerusalem. Comrades, don't be satisfied with your discharge, and your G. A. R. badge, honorable as they are; but live such a life, that when the stars fall, and the rivers cease to sing, you will hear the welcome call: "Come up higher."

There are battles to be fought in the on-coming days, and the promise is to him that overcometh.

There is a day of settlement. When? After

death. "It is appointed unto man once to die, and afterward the judgment." True loyalty never dies.

Dr. Duff, better known as the friend of India, while pleading his cause in 1867, in Edinburgh, fainted and fell. His brethren took him up, and carried him into an adjacent room; and when he revived, he said: "Take me back. I was pleading for India. They shall know that I would die for their interests. Let me finish my plea."

So the soldier sings:

> "Ne'er think the victory won,
>   Nor lay thine armor down;
> The work of faith will not be done,
>   Till thou obtain a crown.
>
> "Fight on, my soul, till death
>   Shall bring thee to thy God;
> He'll take thee, at thy parting breath,
>   Up to his blest abode."

The flag, to a true patriot, is most sacred, and its defence is the patriot's delight.

How could Barbara Fritchie have immortalized her name as she did by her daring defence of the flag, in Fredericktown, while Stonewall Jackson's army was passing through the place? Said she: "Fire at this old, gray head, but spare the flag." To her, it was more precious than life. So with the Prussian officer, who, when found by his enemy, who would gladly have removed him to more comfortable quarters, begged to be permitted to die as he was; for he had secured the regimental flag, and, folding it under his dying form, was holding it from the enemy.

Such should be the feeling of every Christian, in reference to the name of Jesus, and the cross.

Every oath is like a dagger, sent to the hilt into the Christian's heart. We are set for the defence of the truth, as much as ever James was.

I do not wonder at Mr. Savage's attack upon the Scriptures a short time ago; it is in keeping with his avowed profession. He is set forth for the defence of certain interests.

We are Christian soldiers of the Lord Jesus; for others let us be as earnest.

When Jesus' body was in the tomb, the Jews became alarmed, and went to Pilate, asking for increased guards. Pilate said unto them: "The soldiers are at your service. Go, make the tomb as secure as you can." They doubled the guard. Arn't you glad in your soul to-day that they did their worst?

So we say to every foe that threatens our home: "Do your worst, my dear sir. We have no fear; and the sooner you exhaust all the schemes of hell, and all the devices of men, the better for the race. Our God is leading on through tears, furnaces and tombs, to certain victory. Our weapons are not carnal.

Our heroic leader was so devoted to the welfare of his country as to neglect his own pecuniary interests.

He did not suffer anything to hinder his usefulness. He put out his flag, with a purpose to defend it at any cost.

So, if we believe in the name of Jesus, we have no compromise with sinners concerning it. When asked, as were the students at New Haven, a few weeks ago: "Do you believe in the divinity of Christ?" we are ready to say, "Yes;" and not, "I am not quite persuaded to say that I do." I should as soon think of Sheridan saying: "I am not quite persuaded whether the flag is better than the Southern' rag or not," as to have a converted man say he is not quite persuaded as to the deity of his Saviour. To me it is an incomprehensible mystery. I can understand how some of the boys at Cedar Creek did not turn around when Sheridan met them on the 19th of October, 1864; because he was human, and very likely to fail in the conflict. But I cannot understand how a spirit claiming to have met Jesus in the work of regeneration, can doubt his divine claim. When Gilbert Becket was a prisoner of war, he defended his principles so manfully that the Prince admired him, and released him; and the Prince's daughter, having learned two words in English, started in pursuit of the man who defended his principles. First she cried, "London," by which she secured a passage to that city; then she left that to cry, "Gilbert;" and from street to street she cried, "Gilbert," until she found him, whom she never left until death. Let the church believe fully in a hell to shun, and a heaven to gain, and in Jesus Christ as our only Saviour, and this world can be taken. Such men are sure to use the right weapons, and they won't be a life-time finding out the truth.

Fables sometimes contain great truths. There is a fable associated with the visit of Empress Helena to the Holy Land, in search of the cross. Three crosses were presented; and she called for a corpse, and laid first one, then another, upon the dead form; as the real cross touched the dead man, he moved, and life returned. All we ask is, will this make dead men live ? If so, it must be divine.

In the cathedral at Brussels is a wonderful pulpit, called the "Chair of Truth." It is very skillfully wrought, so as to represent a pulpit in the midst of the tree of life, in which the preacher is represented as speaking in God's stead.

Beneath the pulpit are a man and woman hanging their heads in shame, and hastening from the garden of pleasure. Around the tree is wound the serpent, with head lifted above the pulpit, and mouth open to deny every word uttered; but above the serpent is the Christ-Child, with foot on the serpent's head, ready to bruise it, while His mother stands with Him.

How impressive the picture ! Every pulpit is founded in view of the fact that sin is, and abounds; and the only power that can crush it out is the march of Jesus, the Christ.

Every Christian soldier needs just this, in order that he or she may endure hardness, as a good soldier.

The biscuit will be hard-tack, often; dainties only salt junk, and downy pillows, the rugged rocks. We must fight, bleed, die, if need be. We should have some conscience about spending $20 for luxuries, and then staying away from church, because it costs $6 a year to attend it. Some spend $2 a year for the New York *Ledger*, and ten cents for Sabbath school

Sacrifice—endure hardness, as soldiers. Sacrifice for the cause. That don't mean, how little can I get along with, and not appear mean, how much can I sacrifice, and not wrong my family and creditors? That is not what it means. It don't mean, "My head aches; stay at home; rest a little—worked a little hard this week; need rest to-day; the air of a crowded room is bad; I won't go—couldn't enjoy it if I went."

That is from a worldly standpoint. I must pay my pew rent, if my hat *is* poor; for that is God's money. 1 must pay my missionary money; for God said: "Go into all the world." And shall they go, if I don't help? I must be at church, must fight that battle for Jesus to-day.

Too many of us want to go to heaven on flowery beds of ease, and let others fight to win the prize, and sail through bloody seas.

How we do sing that hymn, and then sit and

tremble a whole evening, because the cross is heavy, and we don't feel eloquent and great.

When Mr. Moody canvassed London, an old lady, eighty-five years old, came and asked for a district, and entered upon her mission with a light heart. That's what we want—men and women not too young, not too old, nor too great, to speak and work for Jesus.

The reward of faithfulness is an hundred-fold. Think of Garfield, and his march from the canal-boat to the White House; and Grant, from the stone-yard to the foremost rank of generals; and every boy in blue has been treated with a parchment you cannot purchase with your gold.

The army of our God offers promotion and honors as far above any earthly rewards, as a boundless eternity overshadows a short-lived existence.

I have seen men in the army of the Lord rise in ten minutes, from the companionship of devils and drunkards, into communion with the Deity, and brotherhood with His Christ, and be given a testimonial of immeasurable worth. Comrades in camp, arise, put on thy strength, and go forth into real conquests for God.

And suffer not your cause to fall into unsanctified hands.

During a severe gale, some years ago, at Portland, the cross was blown from the Catholic cathedral; and hundreds—yes, thousands—rushed to guard it, that no unsanctified hands might touch it. Com rades, brethren, let not unchristian hands disgrace the land you have helped make sacred.

"Thy saints, in all this glorious war,
  Shall conquer, though they die;
They see the triumph from afar—
  By faith they bring it nigh.

"When that illustrious day shall rise,
  And all thine armies shine,
In robes of victory through the skies,
  The glory shall be thine."

GEORGE CROOK

"Oh, without the tears that bedim;
　What! standing and weeping for him—
The soldier—why, this is not he,
　In the long, narrow box, that you see;
Only assigned to a higher post—
　He takes full rank with the upper host."

—BARKER.

"Even when we thought him most our own,
　His crown was nearest to his brow;
And he redeemed his earlier vow,
　And passed, with all his armor on."

—REDDEN.

"His gain exceedeth all our loss;
　We linger on these barren sands—
He is a dweller in the lands
　Bequeathed the soldier of the cross."

—REDDEN.

"One moment stood he, as the angels stand,
　High in the stainless eminence of air;
The next, he was not—to his fatherland
　Translated, unaware."

—MYERS.

CHAPTER VI.

GENERAL GEORGE CROOK.

"Set thine house in order, for thou shalt surely die, and not live."

On Friday morning, March 21, 1890, we were forcibly reminded of the uncertain tenure with which we hold this life, by the sudden death of General Crook, who, seemingly in usual health, full of life, purpose and plan, passed from this life to more active fields of usefulness beyond the hills of time.

His life had been one of intense activity. At an early age, while living in comparative poverty, a congressman asked him if he would like to enter the military school and fit himself for the life of a soldier. After careful consideration and counsel, he returned to thank the donor and accept the situation.

His school life was commendable for care and thoroughness, such as gave him the respect of his teachers and the confidence of the people.

Leaving the United States Military Academy in 1852, he entered upon his life work, and was for a time associated with the Fourth United States Infantry, stationed in California. His activity in Range River and Pitt River expeditions gave him at the beginning of the civil war an appointment as colonel of the Thirty-sixth Ohio Infantry Volunteers. He soon won the command of a brigade in West Virginia and Maryland, where, for bravery at Antietam, he was breveted Lieutenant-Colonel in the United States army. He remained with the volunteer army until 1866, and won many expressions of favor. Then he was mustered out of the volunteer service, commissioned Lieutenant-Colonel in the regular army, and assigned command of the Twenty-third United States Infantry, and stationed within bound of Boise District, Idaho.

His tact in handling Indians soon made him famous. In Arizona, during the uprising of the Indians General Crook achieved many signal victories, and upon the retirement of General Terry, was promoted to the rank of major-general, and put in command of the Department of Missouri, which command he held at the time of his death.

His death came to us as sudden, perhaps, because of his intense desire to live, and his absence from the field of action; but death comes to home as well as battle field. Many a comrade has passed through the trials of poverty, war of shot and shell, to die in his quiet chamber, even in the bosom of friends. Be that as it may:

> "One will be with me—those whose voice
> I long have loved and known—
> To die is not my wish, my choice;
> But I shall not die alone."

General Crook, at the hour of his departure, was planning for campaigns and expeditions that stretched far out into the future. He studiously avoided all extra drafts upon his nervous system, in view of long life. Returning from a play in which was portrayed sin and its influence upon the mind of the guilty, the night before his death, he was so moved as to shed tears, and remarked to a friend: "I wish I had not seen that act; it wearies me; I cannot throw it off." He lived long only by having lived well.

I cannot think for a moment that he feared death, for he was a believer in that philosophy which teaches:

"Death cannot come
To him untimely who is fit to die."

Nay, with his strong desire for long life I have fullest sympathy. Indeed, I believe it the solemn duty of every man "who lives to be useful" to desire and plan for long life. His love of life was not, therefore, a weakness or evidence of self-will, but a desire to accomplish something for the land he loved, as a true patriot. In this Luther and Whitfield erred, in desiring to die. Every man ought to make life worth living—and if he does, the longer that life the better. General Crook saw the needs of his native land, and could not bear to leave his life-work unfinished. This was right and commendable.

When wisdom stretches forth her hands to offer

rewards for good living, she says: "Length of days is in thy right hand," as her most excellent gift, The Bible has no pessimistic philosophy—it never discusses the question, whether life is worth living or not; but always holds out objects of interest, and fields of usefulness for the longest and most intense activity.

The biographers of Lyman Beecher have said of him: "He was so hungry to do the work of Him that sent him, that he seemed sometimes to have little appetite for heaven. And after he was seventy years old, one of his children congratulated him that his labors were nearly over, and that he soon would be at rest. To his son's surprise, the old man quickly replied: 'I don't thank my children for sending me to heaven before God does.' In the lecture room of Plymouth church, just before the end of life, he said: 'If God should tell me that I might choose whether to die and go to heaven, or begin my life over again, I would enlist again in a minute.'"

General Crook was ambitious to be a soldier. This was the high aim of his life, and yet there was not in his nature aught of cruelty or love of conflict. Like General Grant, his whole nature was generous and magnanimous. His treatment of the conquered *Chiricahuas* won him an enviable reputation. All that is cruel in war was softened by the influence of his life; for he made nobler the lives of those under him who carried the sword and the musket.

As early as four o'clock in the morning men began their march around the casket of him as he lay in state in our city; and it is estimated that seven thousand men looked upon the face of the General on Sunday, March 23d. The old man who stood by the casket for several minutes, with streaming eyes, said: "He was my friend. For thirty years I have loved him and followed his career, and have come all the way from Jackson County, Michigan, to look on his countenance once more."

He was by nature a soldier. During the rebellion his field of action was very wide, and his personal relation to the conflicts won for him distinction and respect. His equals in rank esteemed him; his superiors respected him, for with Hannibal—he learned to obey. He never questioned the orders of those who had a right to tell him where to go. He discharged the duties that were assigned to him with a valor and tact such as were peculiar to himself. Courteous and gracious, modest and unostentatious, he moved forward with military propriety and soldierly dignity.

He did not yield a point easily. He knew his men, that they were well drilled; and being a strict disciplinarian, he dared trust them in the crucial moment. In a word, his whole career of thirty years' warfare in the service of the United States, is a brilliant and commendable unfolding of his love for military life, and unquestioned patriotism. One author in speaking of his achievements said: "His pursuit into Mexico and capture of Geronimo and his Apaches is as remarkable as anything in the war history of America. And here in the Northwest where he was best known will General Crook's death be most lamented, and the recollection of his brilliant services will be the longest preserved."

It certainly is a laudable ambition to desire to be a soldier, a defender of the Republic. To share in the conflict of the nation against her enemies, and in defense of her institutions is worthy of the devotion of the best men civilization can possibly produce. What would a nation be without this element? Palsied be the tongue that speaks against the heroes of war, or that is lifted to oppose the institutions for which they fought. Those who sneer at legitimate references to the conflict between the North and the South or say aught against the boys in blue or gray, are unworthy a hearing. They have no conception of what that conflict meant.

I heard a young man of this generation saying that he was tired of hearing, on memorial days, of the immense sacrifice of lives and treasure made by the people in the late Civil War. To all such I offer the following facts as given by the Cincinnati *Commercial:* "It is well enough to freshen up the minds of the boys now and then as to the facts of that war, and what it cost their fathers. It takes but few figures to show that it was one of the greatest and most momentous wars ever waged among civilized people, and, taking into consideration its length, the most destructive, costly, and murderous war ever waged. Look over these dreadful figures, young man, and consider the awful significance of the following facts:

"Official returns show that about 2,653,000 soldiers enlisted during the war in response to the successive calls of President Lincoln, and that of this number 186,097 were colored troops. Reports show that the northern and southern armies met in over 2,000 skirmishes and battles. In 148 of these conflicts the loss on the federal side was over 500 men, and in at least ten battles over 10,000 men were reported lost on each side. The appended table shows that the combined losses of the federal and confederate forces in killed, wounded, and missing in the following engagements were: Shiloh, 24,000; Antietam, 18,000; Stone River, 22,000; Chickamauga, 33,000; McClellan's Peninsula campaign, 50,000; Grant's Peninsula campaign, 140,000; and Sherman's campaign, 80,000. Official statistics show that of the 2,653,000 men enlisted there were killed in battle 44,238; died of wounds, 49,205; died of disease, 186,216; died of unknown causes, 24,184; total, 303,843. This includes only those whose death while in the army had been actually proved. To this number should be added, first, 26,000 men who are known to have died while in the hands of the enemy as prisoners of war, and many others in the same manner whose deaths are unrecorded; second. a fair percentage of the 205,794 men who are put down on the official reports as deserters and missing in action, for those who participated in the war know that men frequently disappeared who, it was certain. had not deserted, yet could not be otherwise officially accounted for; third, thousands who are buried in private cemeteries all over the North who died while at home on furlough.

The nation's dead are buried in seventy-three national cemeteries, of which only twelve are in the northern states. Among the principal ones in the North are Cypress Hill, with its 3,786 dead; Finn's Point, N. J., which contains the remains of 2,644 unknown dead; Gettysburg, Pa., with its 1,967 known and 1,608 unknown dead; Mound City, Ill., with 2,505 known and 2,721 unknown graves; Philadelphia, with 1,909 dead; and Woodlawn, Elmira, N. Y., with its 3,900 dead. In the South, near the scenes of terrible conflicts, are located the largest depositories of the nation's heroic dead.

Arlington, Va., 16,264, of which 4,319 are unknown. Beaufort, S. C., 9,241, of which 4,493 are unknown. Chalmette, La., 12,511, of which 5,674 are unknown. Chattanooga, Tenn., 12,962, of which 4,963 are unknown. Fredericksburg, Va., 15,257, of which 12,770 are unknown. Jefferson Barracks, Mo., 11,490, of which 2,900 are unknown. Little Rock, Ark., 5,602, of which 2,317 are unknown. City Point, Va., 5,122, of which 1,374 are unknown. Marietta, Ga., 10,151, of which 2,963 are unknown. Memphis, Tenn., 13,997, of which 8,817 are unknown. Nashville, Tenn., 16,526, of which 4,700 are unknown. Poplar Grove, Va., 6,190, of which 4,001 are unknown. Richmond, Va., 6,542, of which 5,700 are unknown. Salisbury, N. C., 12,126, of which 12,032 are unknown. Stone River, Tenn., 5,602, of which 288 are unknown. Vicksburg, Miss., 16,600, of which 12,704 are unknown. Antietam, Va., 4,671, of which 1,818 are unknown. Winchester, Va., 4,559, of which 2,365 are unknown.

In all the remains of 300,000 men who fought for the stars and stripes find guarded graves in our national cemeteries. Two cemeteries are mainly devoted to the brave men who perished in the loathsome prisons of the same name—Andersonville, Ga., which contains 13,714 graves, and Salisbury, with its 12,126 dead, of whom 12,032 are unknown. Of the vast number who are interred in our national cemeteries, 275,000 sleep beneath the soil of the southern States, and 145,000 of these rest in graves marked unknown.

The total confederate loss will never be known, but the best estimates place it at about 220,000 men out of 1,000,000 men who served in the rebel armies. They fought during the war on the defensive, among friends, and generally under cover of breastworks of one kind or another, from rifle-pits to regular fortifications, which gave them an enormous advantage. The northern men were obliged to fight exposed, being the assailants, while the rebels fired from behind shelter.

The total number of men furnished to the federal army by the United States during the war, under all calls, was 2,783,523. The total number of col.

ored troops in the northern army was 123,156. The heaviest loss by disease was suffered by the colored troops; while 2,997 died in action and of wounds, the enormously large number of 26,301 died of disease. Among the white troops the proportion of deaths in action and from wounds to the deaths from disease was about as one to two; among the colored troops, as one to eight. Of the colored troops enlisted, one out of every seven died of disease. The proportion among the white troops was one to fifteen. Now that we are brushing up these figures, it will be well enough to remember how many men were furnished by each State, and the following list will show:

Maine............71,745	Ohio............317,133
New Hampshire......74,605	Indiana..........195,147
Vermont...........35,256	Illinois..........258,217
Massachusetts.....151,785	Michigan..........90,119
Rhode Island......24,741	Wisconsin.........96,118
Connecticut.......52,270	Minnesota.........25,024
New York.........455,568	Iowa..............75,860
New Jersey........79,511	Missouri.........108,778
Pennsylvania.....366,326	Kentucky..........78,540
Delaware..........13,651	Kansas............20,097
Maryland..........46,730	
West Virginia.....30,003	Total.........2,653,062
Dist. of Columbia..16,872	

Again, the young men must not forget as they read of the great battles of history, that few of them can compare in magnitude with the great battles of the civil war, and that the battles of the war were the bloodiest in all the history of wars in the proportion of killed to those engaged. Waterloo was one of the most desperate and bloody fields chronicled in European history, and yet Wellington's casualties were less than twelve per cent, his losses being 2,432 killed, and 9,580 wounded, out of over 75,000 men, while at Shiloh one side lost in killed and wounded 9,740 out of 34,000, while their opponents report their killed and wounded at 9,616, making the casualties about thirty per cent.

Of the gentlemen who were at West Point during one period of a cadetship, fifty-six were killed in battle, and, estimating the rate of killed and wounded at one to five, 280 were wounded. From the discovery of America to 1861, in all the wars with other nations, the record gives the deaths in battle of but ten American generals, while from 1861 to 1865, both sides being opposed by Americans, more than 100 general officers fell while leading their triumphant columns. From 1492 to 1861 the killed and wounded upon American soil in all battles, combats and skirmishes, added together, as shown by reports, hardly exceeded the casualties of single battle of the great American conflict.

General Crook was faithful in all things entrusted to him, never using for self-advancement any privilege or opportunity, but always looking for the nation's interests. With instincts gentle and humane, he urged justice for the poor savage who surrendered to him; and was grieved over the controversy and proposed removal of the Chiricahua from Florida to Port Sill, and he will always be remembered, because of his attitude toward the unfortunate Indian, who liked his blunt, honest ways and his manly courage. He believed that the military policy of the government was simply one of destruction; and the maintaining of troops in the southwest at the expense of three million dollars a year was calculated to keep up a reign of terror; and he at once took steps to teach the hostile Apaches the necessity of obedience, and they soon learned that General Crook kept his promises, and considered his word as sacred, whether given to the red man or the white man. He banished white marauders and squatters, who were robbing the Indians, and brought peace to the citizens of Arizona. Believing that our Indian troubles were largely due to broken pledges, dishonest agents, government failures and the rapacity of white settlers, he asked for and secured control of the Apaches for two years, during which time there was peace, and I believe but for the new complications of the Interior Department peace might have continued.

General Crook's Indian policy is well put by the editor of the *Christian Union* in these words:

"General Crook's Indian policy was a simple one. His first step was to teach the Indians that they must obey the law. Then they learned that their conqueror invariably fulfilled his promises—often a peculiarly difficult task on account of interference from Washington, and the intriguing and knavery which are usually connected with an Indian reservation. But General Crook did not stop here. His policy was emphatically constructive. It never occurred to him that the Indian question was settled by driving the Indians upon a reservation and keeping them there in idleness with the aid of troops. After conquering the Chiricahuas in 1883, he placed them upon arable land, secured all the farming implements possible, instructed the Indians in their use, and stimulated them by providing a market for their produce. The result was that even the Chiricahua warriors presently became interested in farming, since their work was actually productive and profitable. At the second outbreak in 1885, less than one-quarter of the Chiricahuas could be persuaded by their brethren to leave the reservation. General Crook proved that even the worst Indians prefer peace when they have learned that disobedience is swiftly punished, and that good conduct means the enjoyment of their rights and opportunities to earn money for themselves. Only material arguments like these could be used at first with the wilder Indians.

But they were quick to appreciate the advantages of manual training and of schools, which in General Crook's plan, followed immediately. His plan contemplated the allotment of land in severalty, as a matter of course, as a prime requisite, and in his reports he pointed to citizenship as the goal to be kept always in view. Up to the time of his death he continued, in public addresses and his official writings, to demand justice for the Indians, to expose the abuses of the reservation system and of bureaucracy, and to ask that the Government should grant the Indians independent rights, and give them practical encouragement to become self-respecting, self-supporting beings."

But this work is left for another. May he embody that quality that gained the confidence of the most unruly tribes in our far West. Then shall we have occasion for hope, and

> "Though he has gone to that last bourn
> From which no traveler returns,
> His noble deeds and name will live
> While Freedom's lighted altar burns."

Gen. R. A. ALGER.
EX-COM. IN CHIEF G. A. R.

Peace hath her victories,
　　No less renowned than war.
　　　　　　　　　　—*Milton.*

But whether on the scaffold high,
　Or in the battle's van,
The fittest place where man can die,
　Is where he dies for man.
　　　　　　　　　　—*Barry.*

Their armor rings on a fairer field
　Than the Greek or the Trojan ever trod;
For Freedom's sword is the blade they wield,
　And the light above is the smile of God.
　　　　　　　　　　—*Proctor.*

Along its front no sabers shine,
　　No blood-red pennons wave:
Its banner bears the single line,
　　"Our duty is to save."
　　　　　　　　　　Holmes.

CHAPTER VII.

THE SOLDIER'S ATTITUDE.

Joshua stands in Bible history as a representative warrior. It is true, Moses was a warrior too, but not distinctively so. Likewise Abraham, Ehud, David and Gideon. Still, they do not represent the professional warrior type. They were absorbed with other affairs, and their appearances in battle were phenomenal and unusual. Not that they did not render valuable and efficient service as soldiers. The accounts of the overthrow of the five kings, the forays of Ehud the left-handed, the routing of the robber Midianites by Gideon, and the discomfiture and almost annihilation of Israel's enemies by the shepherd-poet-king, are read and re-read, with ever-increasing interest, even after the lapse of centuries and millenniums.

But Joshua was pre-eminently a soldier. However useful he was in civic and ecclesiastic affairs, however dear he was to Moses and younger Israel, however lofty his virtues, still his chief honor and glory belongs to the military. We might, indeed, say he was the ideal soldier. He was true to his people, to his country, and to his God. Or rather, he was true to God, and was hence necessarily true to his people and to his country. For a man's attitude to his God very largely decides his attitude in every other direction. Joshua was devoted to God, and hence was devoted to his country.

On one occasion Joshua was suddenly confronted by the Lord Omnipotent. Instantly the doughty soldier, with true soldierly instinct and decorum, exclaimed: "What saith my Lord unto His servant?" Napoleon and Alexander and Cæsar never gave utterance to a nobler sentence. The warrior is expected to speak bluntly and to the point, and hence Joshua reaches the very apex of the highest possibility. Meeting the Officer of the Day, the ranking Officer of all the days, suddenly and unexpectedly, his wits do not forsake him. The soldierly instinct is uppermost, and, with proper salutation, he reports for orders: "What saith my Lord unto His servant?"

This is the true position toward God of every true soldierly soul. Joshua, though wise, was not infallible, and, though mighty, was not omnipotent. He recognizes his need of wisdom and strength, and seeks them at the proper place, and the only inexhaustible one. Blessed is that army—soldiers and officers—where the confidence is mutual, and the relations congenial, as between Joshua and God.

There seemed to be, however, in the mind of Joshua, a half-formed doubt as to whether the Being before him was really the God of heaven. But one thought was dominant: "Is this Abraham's and

Jacob's and Moses' Commander? Is this the One who plunged Egypt into mourning on the night of the Exodus? Is this our Pillar and our Cloud? Does he come in Israel's interest? If so, I am ready for orders. Command me, I will gladly obey."

Why did Joshua doubt? Perhaps he was like Thomas—unable to believe without a preponderance of testimony; by instinct and constitution incredulous. Joshua had never seen God in regimentals; he had never seen him accoutred for war; had never come in contact with Him in the role of a warrior. He knew of God as Creator, Preserver and Provider; but as a Captain-General, God was then truly the Unknown God.

Indeed, he had never *seen* God at all. Theophanies had been measurably common to Abraham and Moses, and to others, possibly; but this was God's first appearance to Joshua. Moses was not satisfied without an actual sight of God, and heaven heard him crying: "I beseech Thee, show me Thy glory." The same passion seized the soul of the disciple, Philip, and he exclaims: "Shew us the Father." Give us a glimpse of the ineffable Countenance. Tender was the reply of Jesus: "He that hath seen Me hath seen the Father also." Have you not surmised that I am God? Have I not measured up to your conceptions of the Godhead? Have I not been divinely paternal? "How sayest thou then, 'Shew us the Father?' I and the Father are one."

Ah, God is not angry with the soldier who desires to see his heavenly Commander's face. All heaven is in sympathy with such aspirations. Heaven may not grant the petition now; but the petition itself is sweet with the incense that heaven loves most. To the cry of every soldier's heart for a vision of the Grand Commander's face, innumerable voices answer: "Be patient a little while. Be tender and true. Be Christ-like and pure. Be obedient and unquestioning. The beatific vision awaits you. 'Blessed are the pure in heart, for they shall see God.'" Nor will we ever be satisfied until we see God, face to face, soul to soul. Nor can we ever have the fullness, humanly speaking, of divine knowledge, till we have seen God with our own eyes.

Hence it was fitting in this solemn crisis in the life of Joshua for the heavenly Commander to appear in regimentals—in the accoutrements of war, and give orders for the farther conduct of the campaign. And never was a subordinate more anxious for orders from headquarters. He could no longer turn to Moses, fresh from the senate chamber of heavenly inquiry, for wisdom. There was no human arm upon which he could lean. His hope and help were of heaven.

THE OCCASION OF JOSHUA'S ANXIETY.

Joshua had a tremendous enterprise on his hands. Jericho, a walled city, with impregnable situation—

the Gibraltar of all the surrounding cities and country—lay in his pathway. Like Vicksburg, the Gibraltar of the Mississippi, it was a gateway. It was Joshua's only door of entrance. This valiant, mighty, haughty city must be taken. Nor would she supinely surrender. Joshua knew that one false step, one injudicious movement here, would jeopardise the destiny of millions, if they did not even frustrate the very plans and purposes of Deity. Nor was retreat possible. Fight he must. The Jordan, overflowing and tumultuous, was behind him, Jericho was before him, and the very ground upon which he stood would be hotly contested. He was, indeed, a theocratic king, but he could reign only by grace of arms.

Moreover, his soldiers were in a pitiable condition. They were untrained and undisciplined. They were not inured to the toils and rigors of a military life. The heroes of Egypt and the Red Sea were buried in the wilderness. The younger generation was composed of raw recruits. They were like the farmer-soldiers of Naseby and Marston Moor, of Concord and Lexington. It is not bravery so much that prevents the panic on the field, but discipline. Joshua's untrained and undisciplined host might well have weakened his heart, and filled him with fears of defeat and disaster.

Nor was a lack of discipline all—they were without supplies. The manna no longer fell; covies of quail no more waylaid them. Miraculous supplies mark emergencies, only. God's opportunity perches on the apex of man's extremity, and nowhere else. God deals with us on business principles.

Here were some 3,000,000 refugees, without food or raiment, in a strange land, embroiled in a fierce war, in which one side or the other must suffer extermination. When Lincoln manumitted 4,000,000 slaves, their future maintenance became a grave problem. Yet there was a vast empire open before them, inviting their loftiest endeavors. Still, many of the freedmen no doubt suffered—possibly some of them suffer even yet.

Appalling must Joshua have felt his responsibilities to be. By God's appointment, he was in supreme command—to God was responsible for management or mismanagement, for victory or defeat. Men, under such circumstances, move slowly. When there is no one to share the responsibility, there is little danger of rash and reckless movements. During the last quadrennium the dominant party in American politics often dared fate to do its worst. Why? Because they felt they could shoulder their shame on the Senate. In other words, responsibility was divided. Better have both Houses of the same political complexion. Then responsibility can be located, and there can be no scape-goat to bear away the iniquity of the evil-doers.

Responsibility weighed heavily upon this hero-soldier, and so he cried. "What saith my Lord unto his servant?" I am ready to obey orders, if Thou wilt but condescend to command me. Speak, Lord, for Thy servant heareth. God heard the petition, and granted the prayer. Jericho fell, and God was glorified in the deliverance of His people.

IMPORTANT LESSONS.

Here many important lessons and influences crowd in upon us. One is: *It is ours to know the will of God*. More, it is ours to know even God Himself. This knowledge is of supreme importance. If a knowledge of men is important, as all the world declares, how vital, then, must be divine knowledge—the knowledge of God, and of His mind and purpose. Many false Christs have gone out into the world; like Joshua, we may be able to recognize the true, and not be deceived by the false.

In 1864, Grant ordered my regiment to Sycamore Church and Cox's Mills, near Black Water Station, in front of Petersburg, to guard large supplies there. General Hill, learning of our rich stores there, including 2,500 cattle, charged upon us with his whole division. After a sharp fight, we were ordered to fall back to Sycamore Church, under the protection, as we supposed, of Major Baker, but he and his forces had been captured. As I moved on, with my command, an officer, dressed in our uniform, and entirely familiar with our position and movement, ordered me to advance. I did so, but in a moment was covered with a revolver, and ordered to surrender.

We were fairly duped. This deception cost us all our supplies and hundreds of precious lives, though I escaped, with five men.

But we cannot afford to make mistakes, least of all in the great campaign for eternal life. Nor are serious mistakes necessary—mistakes of a vital sort, —if we know the mind and will and purpose of God. Hence this book, the Bible of the warrior's sainted mother, is our authority on tactics. Follow these instructions and you are safe.

But there are those who claim to have but little need for this book; they receive instructions in all things direct from heaven, and hence the Bible is of but little use to them. Here is great and imminent peril.

I have known men to monopolize the whole time in a testimony meeting, excusing their vaulting pride and selfishness on the ground that they were directed by the Holy Ghost to do so; and leaders to call them to order, under the inspiration, as they said, of the same holy Ghost. Certainly one of the parties was deceived, for the Holy Ghost never antagonizes himself, nor gives contradictory orders to His servants. I instinctively keep my hand on my pocket-book, paralyzed as it is, when in company with men who are so excessively familiar with God, and who claim direct instructions regarding all the trivial affairs of every-day life.

You have probably read of Freeman, a Massachusetts murderer. Heaven commanded him, so he said, as Abraham of old was commanded, to slay his child. And the beautiful, budding life, folded its leaves beneath the chilling kisses of night.

Bismarck is reported to have said that Germany triumphed in the late Franco-Prussian war, because the Germans carried Bibles in their knapsacks. Would that the world were Germanized in this respect. One of the crying needs of the hour is men and women, like the Bereans, fairly devouring the Word of God, and learning daily the will of God. If a man stands squarely on the plain teaching of the sacred volume, he will know the great Commander, and his joy and peace and liberty will be unspeakable. Away with all feelings, impressions and leadings that are not sanctified by the plain utterances of the eternal Word! The Bible is absolutely true to him who is absolutely true to the Bible. Such a man can truly say: "I know that I am right; I know that God knows that I am right; I know that God knows that I know I am right." And, with Job, he may exclaim: "He knoweth the way I take, and when he has tried me, He will bring me forth as gold."

It is always the un-Biblical spirit of cant and compromise that unnerves the believer, and weakens the church of God. There was nothing weak or vacillating about that great martyr, Lincoln. Said he, in the dark days of our awful war: "I want to be sure that we are on the Lord's side; for the Lord is always on the right side.

And to be on the right side is assurance of eventual victory."

> "For right is right, since God is God;
> And right the day must win;
> To doubt would be disloyalty,
> To falter would be sin."

Our Commander always appears at the right time. You are familiar with Holland's great struggle for liberty, when Spain came up against her. Spain, at that time, claimed to be the arbiter of nations and the mistress of the world, and the fate of Holland was apparently sealed. But just at the critical moment God's arm was made bare, and the shackles of political slavery were broken, and the humiliated would-be enslavers were compelled to return home with lowered flags and arms reversed.

It was when Alexander found earth too small for his activities, and tearfully bewailed that there were no more worlds for him to conquer, and Grecian wit and wisdom and art, and Roman power and statecraft were exhausted, and men were sated with life and weary of living, that the great Commander revealed man to man, as the realm of realms, for conquest. It was when Alexander had unified the language of the world by conquest, and Cæsar had unified the nations of the earth by state-craft, and Grecian wisdom, voiced by Plato, the loftiest uninspired mortal that ever lived, declared that if men are to be safely and securely led, there must come a revelation from the Godhead—in short, when the world had reached

Jericho, ready for anything, but not knowing what to do—the great Commander came with seraphic escort, and celestial music, and men and angels hastened with congratulations, and even kings came down from oriental thrones, and in His humble cavernous court, did Him honor and homage.

Here our horizons are rimmed with beaming hope—hope for the individual, for the few, for the many, for all. Our whole life here is a continual Jericho siege with the adversary of our souls. Our enemy fired upon the Sumter of liberty and hope and salvation, not on the 12th of April, but on the 1st of January—upon the first of the first January; yes, before that, when as yet the earth was without form, and void, Satan, "stirred up with envy and revenge," sought the overthrow of God. His pride

"Had cast him out from heaven, with all his host
Of rebel angels; by whose aid, aspiring
To set himself in glory above his peers,
He trusted to have equaled the Most High,
If He opposed; and, with ambitious aim
Against the throne and monarchy of God,
Raised impious war in heaven, and battle proud,
With vain attempt. Him the Almighty Power
Hurled headlong, flaming from the ethereal sky,
With hideous ruin and combustion, down
To bottomless perdition; there to dwell
In adamantine chains and penal fire,
Who durst defy the Omnipotent to arms.
Nine times the space that measures day and night
To mortal men, he, with his horrid crew,
Lay vanquished, rolling in the fiery gulf,
Confounded, though immortal."

Mighty as is our adversary, our Commander is mightier still. Many are the victors: Wellington at Waterloo; Marlborough at Blenheim; Napoleon at Ulin; Cromwell at Marston Moor; Grant at Appomattox; Sheridan at Winchester, and Logan at Atlanta; but our great Commander is the greatest of all. He is the Victor of Victors. He is Hero of Heroes. He is King of Kings.

Often war must precede peace. Many poetize concerning peace, and are forever speaking of Jesus as the Prince of Peace. They appear to think that He will sacrifice everything for peace. Ah, that is one of the devil's fallacies. Never did I have any peace until the battle was fought, and, with self vanquished, and the great Commander triumphant, I ground arms at Emanuel's feet. Then, like Joshua at Jericho, I exclaimed: "What saith my Lord unto His servant;" and, with another: "Speak, Lord, for Thy servant heareth." The way of the cross, is the way of the crown. We lay our treasures up when we lay them down. We triumph when we are conquered. The smiles of peace overspread the war-scarred visage of war. The way to live is to die.

This scene is prophetic of victory. Our great commander still aids the Joshuas who report for orders, and obey them unquestioningly and unmurmuringly. He is the patron of liberty, virtue and righteousness now, as He was in that ancient time. This gives us bases for predicting the moral and spiritual regeneration of all the Dark Continents, both east and west, north and south. Our Commander is marching on, and will continue his victorious progress until He has put all His enemies and all His people's enemies under His feet. Then "the wilderness and the solitary places shall be glad . . . . and the desert shall rejoice and blossom as the rose. It shall blossom abundantly, and rejoice, even with joy and singing."

Herein is assurance. To the trembling Joshua comes the assurance: "See, I have given into thine hand Jericho, and the king thereof, and the mighty men of valor."

"*I have given.*" It is still our Father's good pleasure to give us the kingdom.

> "Rejoice, then, rejoice, all ye people!
> The wondrous transaction is done!
> The life-gate is open; come, enter,
> Through Jesus, the crucified One."

Nor is our tenure of the kingdom brief; no power can wrest it from us.

> "Zion stands, with hills surrounded,
> Zion, kept by Power divine;
> All her foes shall be confounded,
> Though the world in arms combine;
> Happy Zion;
> What a favored lot is thine!
>
> "In the furnace God may prove thee,
> Thence to bring thee forth more bright;
> But can never cease to love thee;
> Thou art precious in His sight.
> God is with thee—
> God, thine everlasting Light."

Weakness, in our great Commander's army, never necessitates failure. He is an inexhaustible Fountain. Are we circumscribed? He is omnipresent. Are we ignorant? He is omniscient. Are we weak? He is omnipotent. He is the full-handed Partner—the unfailing Backer in every Jericho struggle, in every high and holy enterprise. It is but ours to:

> "Watch and fight and pray,
> The battle ne'er give o'er;
> Renew it boldly every day,
> And help divine implore."

Many, I doubt not, have read the journals of the celebrated Charles R. Darwin. In 1832 he made a tour of the world, and on a distant coast discovered a people unspeakably barbarous. They had reached the lowest ebb. To him, they were beyond recovery. Philosophy, science, even religion—all were of no avail, according to Darwin's thinking.

But at that very moment God was planning the rescue of that long-benighted and beastly people—planning, in a mysterious way, His wonders to perform. A parentless, friendless babe was picked up on Thomas street, between the bridges, in Bristol, England. Having no name, he was christened Thomas Bridges—"Thomas" for the street on which he was found, and "Bridges" because found between two bridges. God called him to go to those very people who had so horrified the great Darwin. The church was well nigh faithless in the enterprise; but at last yielded to his burning entreaties, and sent him. He translated the Bible into their language; he preached Jesus; he practiced his heavenly profession, and the tribe was won. England, formerly afraid to land her ships at their shores, now opened up communications, and even Darwin became a patron of those foreign missions. How were they saved? By liberal doses of a Christless Christianity? by agnosticism, rationalism or pseudo free-thought? Ah, no! By the simple story of our great Commander, and the Christly life of the missionary.

God help us, comrades, in life's great and rapidly-closing campaign, to both tell the story and exemplify it in our daily lives. And to our great Commander, the Lord God Omnipotent, we will give all the glory, for:

> "When that illustrious day shall rise,
> And all Thine armies shine,
> In robes of victory through the skies.
> The glory shall be thine."

If solid happiness we prize,
  Within our breast the jewel lies;
    And they are fools who roam;
  The world has nothing to bestow;
  From our own selves our joys must flow,
    And that dear hut our home.

—*Cotton.*

Earth has more awful ruins—one lost mind,
Whose star is quenched, hath lessons for mankind
Of deeper import than each prostrate dome,
Mingling its marble with the dust of Rome.

There is an hour when vain remorse
First wakes in her eternal force;
When pardon may not be retrieved,
When conscience will not be deceived.

—*Hemans.*

GENERAL SHERMAN.

GENERAL SHERMAN.

CHAPTER VIII.

SHERMAN.

Now Jehosaphat slept with his fathers, and was buried with his fathers in the city of David.—2 Chron. 21: 1.

William Tecumseh Sherman was truly a great man, true friend, brave soldier, skilled leader and loyal citizen. Such men never die! A mystic tie gives evidence of their immortality. Alexander, Cæsar, Hannibal, Philip, Xenophon, Frederick, Napoleon, Nelson, Grant, Sheridan and Sherman have disappeared from off the stage; some long ago, others but yesterday, who still seem to live. Yea! they do live! The armies are disbanded and many of the men are numbered among the dead; but these men, like the patriots of Greece and the leaders of civilization, "cannot die." Grant emerging from the Wilderness with the always heroic army of the Potomac; Sherman sweeping through Georgia like a cyclone eight miles wide; Sheridan with his horse on fire shooting like a thunderbolt, reversing the order of the day at sun-down—are to abide with this people through time.

Sherman, in some respects, had no peers. He was born a soldier; like Lincoln, he pleased the masses, but unlike him, he did not please the politicians. He could never be elected on a national ticket because he was too blunt in speech, too resolute in spirit, too independent in thought to be led or lead unorganized men. I once heard a man say of his son's failure to secure the prize for which he had contended: "My boy got the crowd, but the other fellow got the judges"—hence the prize was awarded to the other boy. So with Sherman,—he was in the army for business. The citizen said:

"General Sherman was, taken all in all, the most picturesque military figure on either side of the Civil war, excepting, perhaps, Stonewall Jackson—a soldier he greatly resembled in many characteristics. He was "the beloved of damsels and of dames," as well as of the soldiers and the children. Occasionally, from the worldly standpoint, imprudent in expression, the people respected him all the more because he had what is called "the courage of his convictions." He was a fierce partisan, but never brought his partisanship into social relations, and one of those who most deeply mourned him was that Southern knight with whom he crossed swords so often, and who finally surrendered to him, Joseph E. Johnston."

The principal events of his life are set forth in the following sketch:

He was born at Lancaster, Ohio, February 8th, 1820. At sixteen years of age he entered West Point Military Academy, graduating four years later the sixth in a class of forty-two members. He received his first commission as second lieutenant July 1, 1840, and was promoted to a first lieutenantcy in 1841. In 1846, at the beginning of the Mexican war, he was sent to California. Returning to Washington, in 1850 he married Ellen Boyle Ewing, whose father was then Secretary of the Interior. From 1853 to 1859 he was out of the army, being successively manager of a bank at San Francisco, New York agent of a St. Louis firm, a lawyer at Leavenworth, Kansas, and superintendent of the Louisiana State Military Academy.

He began his career in the army in command of a brigade in Tyler's division. In 1861 he was made a brigadier general of volunteers, and soon became first in command of the troops in Kentucky. At the battle of Shiloh Sherman was wounded in the hand, but refused to leave the field. General Halleck said with reference to that engagement that "Sherman saved the fortunes of the day." Later he was ordered to Memphis, and was made brigadier general on account of his brilliant services in the Vicksburg campaign. In October, 1863, he was sent to the relief of Rosecrans at Chattanooga, and about the same time relieved Burnside, at Knoxville. In April he moved against Atlanta with 99,000 men and 254 guns, the Confederate army under Johnston numbering 62,000 men. In September the enemy evacuated Atlanta, after numerous attacks by Union forces. Then Sherman captured Savannah, having marched three hundred miles in twenty-four days through the heart of Georgia, and achieved a splendid victory. "Sherman's march to the sea" was opposed as chimerical by many of those in authority when it was first proposed. As soon as he finally obtained permission to make the march he ordered the wires cut for fifty miles between Atlanta and Washington. An attempt was later made by the Federal authorities to countermand the order permitting the march, but Sherman of course could not be reached by telegraph. Grant's book states that "the rebels had cut the wires." Leaving Savannah, Sherman captured Charleston, Columbus and Goldsboro. Until 1869 he was in command of the military division of the Mississippi. When Grant was appointed general of the army, Sherman was promoted to be lieutenant general, and when Grant became president of the United States, Sherman succeeded him as general. In 1884, at his own request, he was placed on the retired list, with full pay and emoluments. For some time General Sherman resided in St. Louis, but for a number of years had made his home in New York, where he was a great social favorite. His wife died a few years ago, and his present family in New York consists of two unmarried daughters and a son, besides whom two married daughters and another son survive him.

Such a record is worthy of study, for it shows the possibilities that are within the reach of men. Some say it is a great thing to be born at the right time and in the right place. True! for much depends upon the environments into which men are thrown. It was of immense value to Sherman that he was born in the first quarter of the nineteenth century, and that he came into light in Ohio, through which great surging tides of thought were passing. But remember: he was not the only boy baby born in Ohio in 1820. Where are his associates? Wm. T. Sherman was not the product of circumstances alone,—he was a perfect embodiment of energy. Perhaps the greatest characteristic of this man was his indomitable energy. When in command of the army he was tireless as a worker. Service upon his staff was not arduous, for he rarely called upon any one to assist him. He attended to nearly all his heavy correspondence and read extensively of books relating to his profession, besides maintaining an intimacy with standard and current literature. In addition to this and his social duties he found time to prepare and give to the public his memoirs, which were printed in two volumes in 1875. They dealt almost entirely with the Civil War, and gave rise to much discussion among army men and others, for in literature as in conversation the warrior made no attempt to soften his language or mellow the facts. He followed the old-time maxim, "Hew to the line; let the chips fall where they will." As the result, those struck by the chips cried out lustily. General H. V. Boynton, soldier and newspaper writer, followed with a review of the memoirs, in which he attempted to show where the General was wrong.

In the preface to the first edition of his work, General Sherman used the following language: "Nearly ten years have passed since the close of the Civil War in America, and yet no satisfactory history thereof is accessible to the public; nor should any be attempted until the Government has published and placed within the reach of students the abundant materials that are buried in the War Department at Washington. These are in process of compilation, but at the rate of progress for the last ten years it is probable that a new century will come before they are published and circulated with full indexes to enable the historian to make a judicious selection of materials. What is now offered is not designed as a history of the war or even as a complete account of all the incidents in which the writer bore a part, but merely his recollection of events corrected by reference to his own memoranda."

He saw at a glance that the Civil War was more than a ripple playing over the surface of the nation's life; but that conviction, deep prejudices of long standing were sure to rend the nation unless the people arose in their might. He was pronounced a visionary enthusiast when he said it would take 200,000 men to hold the border States, and some went so far as officially to pronounce him a lunatic. When he grasped the real weakness of the Confederacy and marched from Atlanta to the sea, he became a hero. Nearly all great men hedge themselves about with stage dignity, but Sherman was the one eminent man who could be simply Sherman, and not detract anything from his reputation or dignity.

One story which General Sherman told gives the inside history of the famous March to the Sea. He had been importuning General Grant, President Lincoln and the War Department every day for permission to cut loose from his base of supplies and march through the country from Atlanta to the coast. Stanton thought he was foolish; Lincoln was afraid he'd lose his army; and while General Grant in the main agreed with the plan, there were staff influences around him which were hostile to its execution. One day Sherman received a telegram from Lincoln saying he might use his discretion. He instantly ordered one of his staff to take a detachment and tear down the wires for fifty miles between Atlanta and Washington. This circumstance he never told publicly, but he said that when General Grant's book was published he was interested in a statement which it contained to the effect that General Rawlins went to Washington to countermand the order permitting Sherman to march to the sea, but he found that "the rebels had cut the wires."

His eager spirit was sometimes restless under the restraints put on him by others in authority failing to see and realize the magnitude of the war. His letter to his brother John, written from Memphis, Tenn., August 13, 1862, gives a clear insight into his nature:

"*My Dear Brother:* I have not written to you for so long that I suppose you think I have dropped the correspondence. For six weeks I was marching along the road from Corinth to Memphis, mending roads, building bridges, and all sorts of work. At last I got here and found the city contributing gold, arms, powder, salt, and everything that the enemy wanted. It was a smart trick on their part, thus to give up Memphis, that the desire of gain to our Northern merchants should supply them with the things needed in war. I stopped this at once and declared gold, silver, treasury notes and salt as much contraband of war as powder. I have one man under sentence of death for smuggling arms across the lines and hope Mr. Lincoln will approve it. But the mercenary spirit of our people is too much, and my orders are reversed, and I am ordered to encourage the trade in cotton, and all orders prohibiting gold, silver and notes to be paid for it are annulled by orders from Washington. Grant promptly ratified my order, and all military men here saw at once that gold spent for cotton went to the purchase of arms and munitions of war. But what are the lives of our soldiers to the profits of the merchants? After a whole year of bungling, the country has at last discovered that we want more men. All knew it last fall, as now, but it was not popular. Now

13,000,000 (the General evidently intending only 1,300,000) men are required, when 700,000 were deemed absurd before. It will take time to work up these raw recruits, and they will reach us in October, when we should be in Jackson, Meridian, and Vicksburg. Still I must not growl.

"I have purposely kept back, and have no right to criticise, save that I am glad that the papers have at last found out that we are at war, and have a formidable enemy to combat. Of course I approve the confiscation act, and would be willing to revolutionize the government so as to amend that article of the constitution which forbids the forfeiture of lands to the heirs. My full belief is we must colonize the country de novo, beginning with Kentucky and Tennessee, and should remove 4,000,000 of our people at once south of the Ohio river, taking the farms and plantations of the rebels. I deplore the war as much as ever, but if the thing has to be done let the means be adequate. Don't expect to overrun such a country or subdue such a people in one, two, or five years. It is the task of half a century. Although our army is thus far south, it can not stir from our garrisons. Our men are killed or captured within sight of our lines. I have two divisions here —mine and Hurlbut's—about 13,000 men; am building a strong fort, and think this is to be one of the depots and bases of operations for future movements. The loss of Halleck is almost fatal. We have no one to replace him. Instead of having one head, we have five or six, all independent of each other. I expect our enemies will mass their troops and fall upon our detachments before new re-enforcements come. I can not learn that there any large bodies of men near us here. There are detachments at Holly Springs and Senatobia, the present termini of the railroads from the South; and all the people of the country are armed as guerrillas. Curtis is at Helena, eighty miles south, and Grant is at Corinth. Bragg's army from Tripoli has moved to Chattanooga, and proposes to march on Nashville, Lexington and Cincinnati. They will have about 75,000 men. Buell is near Huntsville, with about 30,000 men, and I suppose detachments of the new levies can be put in Kentucky from Ohio and Indiana in time. The weather is very hot, and Bragg cannot move his forces very fast; but I fear he will give trouble. My own opinion is that we ought not to venture too much into the interior until the river is safely in our possession, when we could land at any point and strike inland. To attempt to hold all the South would demand an army too large even to think of. We must colonize and settle as we go South, for in Missouri there is as much strife as ever. Enemies must be killed or transported to some other country.

"Your affectionate brother,
"W. T. SHERMAN."

He was a man of positive convictions. In January previous to the attack on Sumter he sent in his letter of resignation as President of the Louisiana

State Military Academy, which he held that time at a salary of $5,000. I quote from that letter: "Recent events foreshadow a great change, and it becomes all men to choose. If Louisiana withdraws from the Federal Union, I prefer to maintain my allegiance to the old Constitution as long as a fragment of it survives, and my longer stay here would be wrong in every sense of the word. In that event I beg that you will send or appoint some authorized agent to take charge of the arms and munitions of war here belonging to the State, or direct me what disposition shall be made of them. I beg you to take immediate steps to relieve me as Superintendent the moment the State determines to secede, for on no earthly account will I do any act or think any thought hostile to or in defiance of the old Government of the United States."

This conviction made him naturally and instinctively a soldier. He believed the Rebellion to be treasonable and treated it as such, and he never found forgiveness at the hands of the Southern people. His convictions saved him at all times. In '84, when they pressed him to become a candidate for the Presidency, he positively declined, saying:

"I know the experience of Jackson, Harrison, Grant, Hayes and Garfield made them Presidents, but the civilians of the United States must take this thankless office and leave us old soldiers to take the peace we fought for and earned."

The St. Louis *Globe-Democrat* says:

"The record of General Sherman's military services is specially commended to grateful appreciation by reason of the fact that at all times, as long as he lived, he insisted that there were two sides to the war, one of which was thoroughly right and the other altogether wrong. He did not treasure any resentment against those who tried to dissolve the Union, but he maintained from first to last that the undertaking was without reasonable provocation and in violation of the principles of justice, morality and humanity. When peace came he did not forget how the war had been brought on, and with what desperation the life of the Nation had been assailed. He was willing to forgive the offense, but not to concede anything in its justification. His sense of patriotism was so deep and abiding that he could never find an excuse for the loss and grief, the bloodshed and suffering, that came to pass through the efforts of the South to destroy the government. He never asked that punishment should be inflicted upon those who were responsible for the rebellion and its calamities; like a true soldier he was magnanimous, and the condition of the Southern people at the close of the contest appealed to his sympathy with peculiar force and tenderness. But at the same time he never hesitated to place the blame where it belonged and to say that the South invited the misfortunes by which she was finally overwhelmed.

"This fact is worth remembering in the season of

mourning over the old hero's death. It conveys a lesson that we need to keep constantly in mind and to impress upon the rising generation. The theory that the war involved nothing more than a dispute about doubtful points, and that the two sides were equally right in their respective ways, is a falsification of history. There were no questions of mere expediency to be determined; the struggle was one in which principles were at stake, and when it ended certain things were established that had vital and splendid meaning. The fact that the Southern armies did valiant fighting is to be acknowledged, but it is not necessary to say that they fought thus because they were inspired by the same high sentiments that animated the Union armies. There was a distinct and significant difference between the two in that respect, and we cannot afford to lose sight of it on any account. One side was defending the Nation against a wicked attack on the part of the other, and it is useless to say that both had the same degree of loyalty and integrity to sustain and vindicate them. The matter is not one to be discussed in any spirit of enmity. It is simply a great historic truth to be recognized and perpetuated in our political philosophy. The North was right and the South was wrong, as Sherman always declared; and any view of the war which divides its honors in even measure is contrary alike to the demands of common justice and the teachings of common sense."

Many of the Southern papers have commented on Sherman's death in a spirit of fairness; some of them have spoken appreciatively of him as one of America's greatest soldiers; but the Columbus (Ga.) *Sun* says:

"In his operations in this State, he concentrated all the brutalities and called up all the horrors of war. But it was largely old men, women and children who trembled and fled before the sword and torch which he upheld. The brutal treatment of helpless people, the ashes of Atlanta, and the devastation and desolation that marked his march to the sea, were the records of his prowess as a soldier. It was barbarism, but he said it was war. It was war, but in summing up the character of the man who inaugurated it, Georgians cannot forget it, nor give him praise for it. His policy was not the policy of that greater soldier, whom the North idolized and the South forgave."

"Forgave," indeed! Did the woman who was told to go in peace and sin no more forgive her absolver? When the helpless, hopeless, hungry South surrendered without truce or terms, when Grant dismissed its erring, but valiant, soldiery to their homes upon the one condition that they should return, resume their plows and their trades, "not to be molested so long as they obeyed the laws and Constitution of the United States," was it expected that in less than the lifetime of a man the whole South again should bid open defiance to the laws and Constitution, and should boast that in 1865 it "forgave" its conqueror?

The terms granted by Sherman to Johnston's soldiers were even more magnanimous than those which Grant gave to Lee's. The lately departed General of the Armies of the Nation was as tender in peace as he was strong in war. The South never had a better friend than Sherman, never will have. We regret such demonstrations as several of the Southern journals have made concerning the death of Sherman. We regret them exceedingly. We regret all Southern dissensions from that perfect nationality which is evidently the recognition and enforcement of "one law, one element," in all parts of the country. There cannot be two paramount policies in two sections of the Nation. That which hath been is that which shall be; the doctrine of the widest freedom and the deepest loyalty to the Nation ultimately will prevail in all the States. This was Sherman's creed, it is ours, and it is the creed of the North, though the South may not believe so. The South did not believe that the creed of the North was National, until the dreadful voice of the sword announced it.

With this, which sometimes made him appear unkind and severe, Sherman was social and kindheartedness itself. A New York editor says:

"After his retirement General Sherman became a social lion. His engagements would long ago have worn out a man of ordinary mold and make, but the veteran of a hundred campaigns entered his new life with the keen zest and endurance of an iron constitution. His ready though occasionally caustic wit, his entertaining personal reminiscences, and developed talent as raconteur and after-dinner speaker made him much sought. Compliments and attentions, even flattery, were showered upon him, and the latter days of the seamed old warrior were his most delightful. All his social triumphs seemed only to accentuate his democratic and at the same time soldierly ways and habits of expression. His moods, when he had the cares and responsibilities of office upon him, were variable. At times he was severe and at others the gentlest, mildest, most warm-hearted of men. During the last eight years his nature took its natural bent and his finer qualities became wholly predominant. Blunt and honest to a marked degree, actions often ascribed to a harsh disposition were but the result of General Sherman's inability to clothe his refusals of favors requested or his commands in the purple and fine-linen language of the courtier. He went straight for a point and achieved it without much choosing of words. He had such an utter, manly and characteristic contempt for ordinary diplomacy that it is doubtful whether he ever attempted to conceal his views, however radical they may have been. He is one of the few public men of the last quarter of a century who had the courage of his convictions and was wholly free from fear in his expressions."

GIVING AWAY HIS SECRETS. 161

Again, he never failed to see the fitness of things. On one occasion he had halted for rest on the piazza of a house by the roadside, when it came into the mind of an old Confederate who was present that he might pick up a bit of valuable information by careful quizzing. He knew by Sherman's dress that he was an officer, but had no suspicion as to his rank. When he heard a staff officer use the title of "General" he turned to Sherman in surprise and said: "Are you a General?"

"Yes, sir," was the response.

"What is your name?"

"Sherman."

"Sherman? You don't mean General Sherman?"

"That's who I mean."

"How many men have you got?"

"Oh, over a million."

"Well, General, there's just one question I'd like to ask, if you have no objections."

"Go ahead."

"Where are youns a going to go when you go away from here?"

"Well, that's a pretty stiff question to ask an entire stranger under these circumstances, but if you will give me your word to keep it a secret I don't mind telling you."

"I will keep it a secret; don't have no fear of me."

"But there is a great risk, you know. What if I should tell you my plans, and they should get over to the enemy?"

"I tell you there is no fear of me."

"You are quite sure I can trust you?"

"As your own brother."

The General slowly climbed into the saddle and leaned over to the expectant Confederate, who was all eyes and ears for the precious information. "I will tell you where I am going. I am going—just where I please." And he did, and there was not power enough in the South to stop him.

He never forgot the boys. When on his campaigns his habits were of the simplest. He arose early and was up late at night. In the face of the enemy his regular ration of sleep was five hours. Reveille often found him in the saddle and out on the most exposed parts of his front. The orders were that he should be aroused at any hour of the night to receive reports. In the Atlanta campaign he set the example of discarding tents and reducing baggage to a minimum. There was but one tent at headquarters, and that was used by the Adjutant-General and his clerks. Sherman and his staff slept on the ground under a tent-fly, which was stretched over a pole resting in the crotches of convenient saplings. It was often said that Sherman's headquarters were in a candle-box, as all his papers were carried in one of these homely receptacles which had been emptied of its original contents. The soldiers knew him affectionately as "Old Tecump." His middle name, "Tecumseh," was given him by his father, who, in the war of 1812, had conceived a great admiration for the Shawnee war-chief.

"Uncle Billy" was the name by which he was generally known in the army during the March to the Sea. He had but a single sentry at headquarters; but no one, whether officer or private, who desired speech with the General was stopped. He always had a cordial and encouraging word for the men when he rode along the line in front of the enemy or when a moving column passed him. For the details of military etiquette and ceremony he had slight care; from him promptitude and steadiness in action and endurance in marching always evoked praise. Unless his plans required secrecy he was free and outspoken in his communications, and this very frankness often deceived the enemy and misled him as to Sherman's intentions.

He never forgot the little drummer boy who came to him in the hot fight at the rear of Vicksburg, and when it came in his power he had the youngster appointed to the Naval Academy at Annapolis. The troops were in the heat of the engagement, when Sherman heard a shrill, childish voice calling out to him that one of the regiments was out of ammunition, and that the men would have to abandon their position unless he sent to their relief. He looked down, and there by the side of his horse was a mite of a boy, with the blood running from a wound in his leg.

"All right, my boy," said the General, "I'll send

them all they need, but as you seem to be badly
hurt, you had better go and find a surgeon and let
him fix you up."

The boy saluted and started to the rear, while
Sherman prepared to give the required order for
the needed ammunition. But he once more heard
the piping voice shouting back at him: "General,
caliber fifty-eight! Caliber fifty-eight!" Glancing
back, he saw the little fellow, all unconscious of his
wound, running again toward him to tell of the
character of the ammunition needed, as another size
would have been of no use, and left the men as
badly off as before. Sherman never could speak
too highly of the little fellow's pluck; he asked him
his name, complimented him, and promised to keep
an eye upon him, which he did. He often related
the story, and always with praises for the little soldier's bravery.

Comrades, we have lost a true friend who was a
typical American, a great soldier, a born leader, an
intelligent general, a true patriot and a loyal citizen.
He had untiring energy and restless activity. In
defeating Johnston he defeated the man whom history will proclaim as the greatest general of the
South. Alexander never succeeded better and
Napoleon never outstripped him. The peerless
Logan looked up to him as an intelligent leader.
He was a giant intellectually, one of those American
products of which all are justly proud. He was a
man of mighty convictions. He was loyal to the

end of his life. Such men should have a place in the hearts of all for years to come. We who are left behind should not go to the mountains to look for the bones of those who have fallen, but take up the mantles of the departed as Elisha did of old, and go on with the work, so as to be ready for the roll-call when summoned to the encampment on high.

CHAPTER IX.

WILLIAM TECUMSEH SHERMAN.

BY OLIVER O. HOWARD, MAJOR GENERAL, UNITED STATES ARMY.

(Published at the time of his death in the New York *Independent*.)

My own relationship to General W. T. Sherman has been such that it is difficult to speak or write of him as I would of any other officer with whom I have been associated. It was regarded by me, and I think by him, more like that of father and son than of general and subordinate. This relationship was only incidental while we were both commanding brigades under Generals McDowell and McClellan in the early part of the war. I read of him after he went West, saw the grand plans that he insisted on, plans of large scope and demanding more men than any other dared to ask; so much so that those who traduced him and General Grant on account of the first day's disaster at Shiloh, took advantage of the apparent extravagance and tried to make the country think that he had become delirious. True, nobody believed it, nobody in places of responsibility; but the reports nevertheless wounded Sherman, who was always exceedingly sensitive under aspersion. Aspersion never drove him from a course of conduct that he deemed wise and best; but cruel accusers can have the satisfaction of knowing that they succeeded in hurting a sensitive heart—a satisfaction that must be delightsome to cold-blooded malignity.

The fact is that Sherman having been located in Louisiana at the outbreak of the war, and being intimately associated with numerous public men, knew at once what was coming when the resistance of the conspirators found its starting point at Fort Sumter. He, in his capacious mind, measured the length and breadth and far-reaching scope of the well-laid plan and the practical measures to sustain it, which years of secret discussion had finally brought into exceeding completeness. So when he came North, visited General Scott, President Lincoln and Cabinet officers near the outbreak of the Rebellion, he impressed them greatly, but was so optimistic and prophetic of large undertakings and great consequences that they, following their hopes rather than the facts, imputed to him exaggeration.

Time justified all his predictions. I knew of these things. He appeared to me quite early meteoric in his action and doings; but I had not come in personal contact with him to any extent until we met at Chattanooga after Rosecrans' defeat of Chickamauga, and during Grant's and Thomas' preparation in that little besieged nook half encompassed by the Tennessee River, when Longstreet sat upon the top of Lookout and Bragg upon Missionary Ridge only waiting like birds of prey to swoop down upon the remnants nearly ready for their consumption.

You should have seen Sherman when he first appeared at Chattanooga. It is a scene that I have often described—an upper room; present Grant, Sheridan, Thomas, Gordon Granger, and a few other prominent men. Sherman had just arrived ahead of his troops, his column, the old Army of Tennessee, coming from the Mississippi. He bounded into the room with joyous heartiness.

"How are you, Grant?"

"How are you, Sherman? Take the high-back chair."

"No, Grant, that is for you."

But Grant must give it to age.

"Well, if you put it on that ground, I must accept."

So he takes the chair and the offered cigar, and then instantly commences that singular flow of pregnant words so magnificently described by Mr. Depew in one of the morning journals. No one ever heard military plans more thoroughly sifted, objections being made and answered, than on that night. Then was revealed to my eyes the character of each model before me. I realized Sheridan's vigor, something of Thomas' completeness of research and fixedness of purpose, of Grant's universality of acquirement and clear-cut judgment. But I thought then, Sherman is eccentric; he is different from the rest; he is quick as lightning; he is a genius.

Subsequent experience only confirmed me in my estimate of the man. He had no equal in strategic combinations, for a quick comprehension of his enemies' plans and locations, even in a blind forest country, for rapid changes, adapting himself at once to a new situation in a campaign, as when he decided and did reorganize his own force for the march to the sea and through the Carolinas, and sent the sturdy Thomas forthwith to Nashville, supporting him by such men as A. J. Smith and J. M. Schofield, and other successful and energetic commanders. His projects were approved, and they were executed to the letter; and surely through this planning and execution the Confederacy received its disabling if not its mortal wound.

A friend this morning, speaking of the hope that General Sherman might yet recover, for he was only seventy-one, I could not help answering: "Sherman is older than that." Yes, age in such times as we have been through cannot be reckoned by years. Think of the strain of the spring campaign of 1864, when the whole Western responsibility was thrown upon Sherman, Grant having gone to stay by the Eastern force; for fifteen days under fire every day, with only three days' intermission, under fire of artillery, and very often within range of the enemy's rifles. He was constantly on the *qui vive*, using his whole mind. He slept, it is true, but never long at a time.

You are doubtless acquainted with the incidents at Resaca, a two days' battle. Early in the morning, as the troops were moving into position in columns, a rough soldier, noticing some officers lounging near a large log, and Sherman sitting upon the log with his head drooping, seems to have fancied that he had been drinking, and called out quite plainly to a companion: "That is the way we are commanded," or something like it. Sherman, hearing the remark, made the soldiers stop, and said to them, with his usual vigor of style: "While you were sleeping, I was awake making plans and conducting correspondence, and now I was just taking a little needed rest." You may imagine how ashamed the men were as they marched on to do their important work, but work not so trying to the strength or exhausting to the system as that of their commander. Generally there was a strong, abiding faith in Sherman's ability. It did not show itself so much as with Sheridan, Thomas and Grant in the battles, but in his comprehensive grasp of the whole situation.

Sherman must have studied at some time of his life with great assiduity, he must have been reading while others were sleeping, for his knowledge, both scientific and historic, was certainly marvelous. General Blair and I, as we passed through the Carolinas, would undertake to recall a Revolutionary battle as we passed from one historic point to another. We would have confused recollections of such a field as the Cowpens, for example. Blair would say to me, laughingly: "Well, Howard, we can settle it by going to Sherman. He knows it all." And indeed he did. I noticed once, as we were approaching Marietta, with General J. E. Johnston between us and that point, the enemy's field being still beyond a range of hills, how Sherman began to evolve his plans. He came over to my bivouac of an evening, and told me in a running conversation, with an occasional use of his pencil, of the entire situation and surroundings of Marietta, of the roads, of the hills, of the river, mapping out to me a detail such as a reconnoitering officer would have given if there had been no enemy there, and he had had a favorable opportunity for a complete survey.

I said: "How do you know all this, General?"

"Oh, when I was a young man I was stationed at Charleston for a while, and I traveled over this country."

Twenty years' interval had not blotted from his mind the topographical features of the river valley. It indicated, of course, the habit of intense observation.

Sometimes the General, during our campaigns, would ride for hours without speaking a word, occasionally dropping his head forward upon his breast as his horse would jog along accompanying other horses without the necessity of the guiding rein. General Grant called that habit of Sherman's "boning," a West Point phrase for intense study.

Yes, this habit of intense thinking prolonged made him live two years in one. He came near breaking down at Atlanta physically. One day I came in and a great numbness had seized one of his arms and shoulders, and an orderly was rubbing him. Then it was that he pointed out to me his hope for the coming campaign; then it was that he put his finger upon Goldsboro, N. C., and said: "That is the point we must reach."

You may ask me what Sherman's genius consisted in. It was like that of Columbus. He saw new continents before they were discovered, and he had the energy to formulate the proper plans and the ability to inspire others with a sufficient enthusiasm for their accomplishment. It was like that of Napoleon, for he comprehended his enemy's abilities at a glance and brought his troops to just the points essential to his discomfiture; and he inspired his lieutenants not only with confidence but with affection; they loved him, and love him still, those who are living, with an affection that Napoleon Bonaparte, with his want of fundamental principle, could never inspire.

Sherman's moral qualities were more developed than his war companions used to think. He never willingly did a tyrannical or unjust act. Of course to a great leader like him the conduct of subordinates was often imputed to himself, and he had much of Grant's magnanimity which led him to bear patiently unjust accusations, but not always. It was natural for him to resent insults and blunt as far as he could the sharp stings of opposition. Once I was near him when an account was given of the last great review at Washington. The speaker closed it as if it ended the day before the Western troops passed the President's stand. This fretted Sherman as such things always would, and so he replied by showing what he deemed to be the superiority of Western troops. He was so worried about this little incident that for a time nearly everybody who came near him received an abrupt rejoinder. In this way he often lost strong personal friends. But there was no depth to his resentments, and they didn't last. He was the quickest to forgive.

Perhaps there is nothing pleasanter to remember than the last two years of Sherman's life here in New York. It has been a review of the past, a rejoicing in the present, and an optimistic prophecy of the glorious future for the country. He delighted to have his two wing commanders by his side—General Slocum and myself. I do not think he ever seemed happier than when we were together. He held General Slocum and General Schofield in very high esteem. He would say of them: "They are capable of large combinations. They are true men."

It is not quite true what we see in the papers at the death of each leader, that the great men of our generation have passed away. History will find many another able leader, many an officer of large brain, of magnificent courage, of quick insight and abundant accomplishment, junior, of course, to the great leaders who have gone, but in many respects and in undoubted genius, Sherman is ahead. He was essential to Grant's singular completeness as a warrior.

CHAPTER X.

WISDOM AND WAR.
By Rev. George H. Corey, D. D.

Wisdom is better than weapons of war.—Eccl. ix. 18.

These words affirm the supremacy of wisdom. Its salutary creations and ministries in the varied spheres of civil, social and moral life, surpass all warlike agencies. Wisdom is superior to force. It does not follow, however, that the weapons of war are useless. They have their place and value, and are efficient for the moral uses to which they are ordained in the discipline and development of the world. War is a dire calamity, involving moral hazard and woe. Stern, stormful, and grim, it has darkened the world with fear and torn it with violence; with bloody heel, it has trampled upon justice, crushed beneficence, destroyed happiness, superseded every law of the Decalogue—ignored every principle of the Beatitudes, and silenced all laws but that of military necessity. But for all that it has its providential place—its beneficent side. Unless we surrender the right of self-preservation and concede that man, abused, crushed, robbed, and despoiled on every hand, must submit without resistance, war is inevitable. We may outgrow the conditions that seem to make a resort to arms necessary, but in the past war has been a civilizer. Following almost every great war there has been a new impulse to progress. In the early ages, when the means of intercommunication were limited, and the art of printing was unknown, nations in close proximity were ignorant of each other. Isolation meant deterioration, decay, death. War brought them together—became a means of intercourse, communication of knowledge, familiarity with each other's homes, institutions, usages, arts, and an interfusion of ideas that lifted raw, brutish people out of their stupor and stagnation to liberty, life, and power. Old conventions and abuses were broken; old prejudices, superstitions, dynasties were sundered; old chains were snapped into fragments. Nations burst their former boundaries, crossed their blood and sharpened their brains, liberalized their judgments and enlarged their experience. In their wild mountain fastnesses the rude Goth and Vandal must have remained a coarse, barbarous people. Undisturbed in her material glory the Roman Empire must have sunk deeper and deeper into luxury, license, and lethargy. But the northern barbarian looked upon the once magnificent, though now effete civilization, and was smitten with its splendor; and he came, a rough bridegroom from the forest, for this southern bride. It was a wild wooing and a fiercer wedlock, but the marriage was pronounced; the domestic doors of Europe swung wide on their rusty hinges; the nations mixed; and although this was effected through invasions, fire and sword, through campaigns, sieges, and slaughters, this mingling of races has given us civilized, cultured Europe. The world could ill afford to spare the fruit of its battles and its revolutions. How terrible was the process of the Greek wars of Alexander in their wide devastations, and how deadly and far the flight of the Roman eagle, with his dire talons, pitiless beak, and imperial ambition. Yet now we see what failed to dawn on their vision— how Alexander and Cæsar were preparing a path for Providence. The Greek conquests furnished the compacting influence that provided readers through the civilized world for the Greek Gospels of the New Testament, and for the Greek septuagent of the Old Testament. The Persian dreamed not of such a result as he rushed westward on Marathon and Salamis. The Macedonian Phalanx had no such thought when it rushed eastward to Arbela. So the Roman invasions and conquests opened the provinces of their world for the message of a higher wisdom. The nations trampled by martial squadrons became the material, compacted under the unity of Hellenic literature and Greek civilization, and the unity of Roman law and polity, for the building of that fairer edifice of Christian civilization upon which God's eye rested through all the turmoil and carnage of those Pagan battle-fields.

So the race that inherits the British Isles were

triturated together, as the painter rubs into unity the colors on his palette, from the days of the Heptarchy down, by the conflicts and agonies of centuries.

The wars that tracked the Protestant Reformation on the soil of Germany, Holland, France, England, and Scotland, and the later struggles of the English Commonwealth, scattered wretchedness and woe on every side, and much that was wrong; but who could well spare from European and American history the deeds of truth and life then sown? The good far outweighed the evil. Could literature, could freedom, could religion forego the heroes, sages, confessors, and martyrs that emerged in those trials, grew wiser and holier in that fiery furnace, and bequeathed to us their inspiring testimony and their enduring trophies? Nay, verily! the world cannot part with the fruit of its bitter struggles. It is doubtful whether human nature can be trusted in profound and unbroken peace and prosperity, with its mortal passions, mortal sluggishness and selfishness, without hostile collisions. Had war never come, centuries would continue to roll away, and in all nations there would be nothing but toil, accumulation, and the multiplication of comfort and luxuries. Poverty, thrift, prosperity, wealth, luxury, effeminancy, dissipation, degradation, death—in these nine words the fate of empires is told. Who shall say, therefore, that war has not its moral uses? The great Napoleon said: "The conscription is the everlasting root of the nation, its moral purification, the real foundation of its habits." I suppose that he meant that the bond of that dread liability which holds every family in a nation to loyalty and love, that will surrender its choicest sons to die for their country, inspires a principle of sobriety, of manliness, of sacrifice, of obedience to the law, of consecration to the commonwealth, which nothing else could impart. How else shall we defend our altars and our homes? How maintain our institutions when assailed? How overthrow deep-seated injustice, repair the waste of intolerable oppression, redeem and purify prevalent corruption, or renew and invigorate a wasting effeminancy? It is far better that the moral sentiments and the material interests of society should be in fierce collision than in a state of paralysis and decay. Believe me, then, however fearful the field of strife and carnage, there is something more grievous to a people than war, than civil war itself, with its appalling progeny of evil. The loss of public virtue, the spread of falsehood, the reign of treachery, the exaltation to places of honor of the illiterate, the vulgar, the sordid and rapacious; the depreciation of manhood and its liberal impulses and grand attributes; the extinction of that faith in its own righteousness and power which is the life of a Nation and which has nerved the smallest State to cope with empires and successfully resist them, and which, as it is ever its ornament of purest gold, never fails to be in the hour of danger its shield of adamant; *these* are evils that far surpass the destructiveness of those to which, even in its most lavish riotousness, war gives birth. The havoc that war makes may be repaired. Industry, art, ambition survive, although wide regions are laid waste. But the desecration of manhood, the corruption of virtue, the enthronement of vicious principles, lead to inevitable and permanent decay. Still, let us remember that war is medicine, not food; it is surgery, not calisthenics; it is judgment, not mercy. Inevitable as I believe it to be in the present constitution of the world, subserving as it has in the past a high moral purpose, I still believe that human society will outgrow it when it outgrows its vices, its angry passions, its injustice, selfishness, and ambition. Till then the world must share its oppression and suffer its cruelty. But let no man say that all war is fruitless; that the world has gained nothing by its fierceness. Let it not be said that nations fight and exhaust themselves, and then negotiate and get by negotiation what they sought by the sword. The past refutes it; our own history disclaims it. In every war we have gained the object for which we engaged in the conflict. The power of the French was broken by our colonial struggle on this continent. The Indians were subdued. We gained the political independence for which our great revolutionary struggle was begun. The war of 1812 yielded the results we sought. In all contests we have gained the supreme end for which we lifted our banner. It seemed to the people of the United States that God had entrusted them with treasures for the good of all mankind which could neither be preserved nor distributed were we to become a shattered nation. For a nation's life we went to war. We brought back that life in full power as our trophy. Orpheus is fabled, in seeking his departed spouse, to have gone down to the regions of the dead, and by his lyre to have won his way, charming every adversary to sleep, and to have brought her forth again to life, light, and love. Not ours was the charming lyre that put all foes to sleep, but with the martial strain mingling with the roar of battle, and the tramp of squadrons that shook the continent, we marched through purgatorial suffering to bring back our lost companions, and we brought them. We made war the instrument of justice, the herald of liberty. When the war is waged for a principle, for benign institutions, then the war-wave rolls with the impetus and weight of an idea and the energy of moral enthusiasm.

Now, this is the great struggle that has erected this memorial service in which we honor the memory of the patriotic dead.

Signal public service rendered to the State and sublime sacrifice for its defence ever command reverent admiration. They kindle the generous ambition of youthful aspirants for public honor. Themistocles could not sleep for the trophies in the

Ceramicus. Yet when such trophies have faded, when the marble urn, the sculptured vase, and the brazen cenotaph have crumbled, and all physical evidences of the existence of the heroes of the past have perished, the story of their heroism shall live in the memory of mankind, for all good men are gifted with a double immortality. Their words, their deeds, their lives, become enshrined in benign institutions which survive all desolation and change. The memory of the wise and patriotic never perish. Leonidas and Miltiades, Cato and Tully, Washington and Lincoln, Garibaldi and Grant, and they our fallen brothers, unknown to fame, but none the less noble, they who fell for freedom's cause, live embalmed in the hearts of mankind, and shall live when bronze and marble have perished—shall live as long as men revere law, honor patriotism, and love liberty. What if no classic urn preserves their dust, it is held in soil rendered forever sacred by their sacrifice. And what if no monument records their names, they are graven an imperishable record on the Nation's heart. Indeed, this annual memorial service so generally observed by our citizens, auspicious omen and generous privilege, has come to be monumental. How gladly do our hearts respond to its annual return, as we meet with gratitude and joy to rekindle our patriotic fervor, and revive the lamp of political hope at the sepulchre of the heroic dead. The hour comes to us freighted with precious thoughts and noble inspirations. If the dead body of Lucretia, planted by the hand of Brutus, brought forth the living liberators of Rome; if the ghastly wounds on Cæsar's manly form, as Antony lifted his shroud, were the seeds whence sprang the tyrants of ten centuries; if an annual oration delivered from its sacred precincts made the tomb of Leonidas yield a yearly crop of heroes, shall the remembrance of our heroic period, with the recital of the deeds that made it glorious, be without corresponding results? Shall the traditions of our heroic struggle fail to find justification in the manhood and in the manifest destiny of our country?

It is a beautiful fact that the record and the memories of our revolutionary strife foster the highest patriotic sentiment. They stir the blood and the brain. They thrill the senses and satisfy the imagination. They quicken the Christian's faith in the reality of principle, in the influence of heroic self-sacrifice, and the power of ideas. For that strife liberated from the shock of steel and the battle's smoke ideas which have since changed the destiny of the world.

And on this sacred day, as we revert to another and a grander struggle, our patriotism must be inspired by the ideas which redeemed those fields from insignificance and pledged us to establish and unfold them in our country, according to the new needs and invitations of the age.

How significant, then, is this annual memorial service! How full of meaning and how sacred its ministries? Every mention of the ideas to which our land is consecrated, and the importance of its mission, calls up the crisis through which we have passed and the dangers with which our institutions were confronted. They revive a new interest in what may be called the heroic period in our national life. They bring before us a period of revolution when our private fortunes, our personal affections, and our political prospects were overcast, torn with doubts and fears, or smitten with blight and ruin. They also show us the newness and the magnitude of the events; the vastness and unexpectedness of the changes; the splendor, and yet the peril, of the opportunities which have opened upon this era. It is no exaggeration to call this more than an ordinary traditional period in human history. It was, indeed, an epoch in the world's social progress; a time of humanity's emerging from chivalric barbarism; a time of rebellion, and yet a time of revolution and reconstruction in the organic laws of the land. From 1860 to 1870—what a sublime period! What a place will it occupy in the history of the world as the great crisis of self government; the awful trial-scene of man's asserted equality before the law, the *experimentum crucis* of free government!

We may not pause now to review that period or gather into our hearts all the lessons it unfolds; but these are among the facts that cannot be overlooked. For eighty years the nation had prospered. Every decade its enemies prophesied its decline, and every decade the figures told how it grew. In national wealth, in commerce, agriculture, and manufactures, in the growth of its cities, springing up as if by magic, in the development of the arts, sciences, literature, it had astonished the world. Its ideas were steadily affecting the policy of nations. The subjects of monarchial and despotic governments were yearning for personal rights. Hereditary legislation and the thrones of haughty imperialism trembled before the expanding power and glory of our democracy. It was secretly kindling the tinder of popular justice, which, smouldering for a time, seemed destined to shatter every throne of royalty.

But, alas! a change came; a dark cloud rose on the southern sky, eclipsing the ascending sun of liberty. In her proud career the nation was suddenly arrested and almost paralyzed with fear by the tread of mighty hosts gathering for the shock of battle. Our people were convulsed with new and strange emotions. Our fertile fields, laughing with harvests sufficient to banquet the world, suddenly became the arena of a sublime controversy—a controversy not merely local, but of universal interest, upon which the whole world gazed, interested, anxious, or affrighted spectators. The cause was worthy the arena and the beholders. It could not have been fitly tried on any smaller field or in any meaner presence. It concerned the human race, and involved the destinies of the world. It was the battle of mankind. It was a quarrel among ourselves, and for no cause less than self-existence; a peril that could spring up only from our own bosoms, could have tested the character and the value of American institutions. What foreign war could have tried the courage, the faith, and the patience of our people as this civil war has done? Against what other foe could we have expended so much treasure and shed so much precious blood? What other war would not have called out chiefly the vulgar and unwholesome passions of our people, commercial and economical rivalries, hatred of race, pride of blood, and the coarse and degrading sentiments that mark the feelings of the Ottoman and the Muscovite? When, in all history, and between what other foes, has a war gone on "more in sorrow than in anger," under a dreadful sense of destiny? Brothers, we must remember the nature of this conflict. It was not in the interests of trade nor the rights of commerce; it was not interest of race nor the breaking out of ancestral grudges; it was not lust of territory nor love of power; it was a contest neither sectional, geographical, nor even political in any partisan sense. But it was in reality a war of principles irreconcilable; of ideas entirely antagonistic; of civilizations diverse which can never be harmonized; of purposes that will not parley, assimilate, nor compromise. In its local form it was a contest between slavery and freedom—in a larger sense it was a contest between democracy and despotism. It offered to us for solution this question: Has liberty power to protect and perpetuate the State she adopts, or is anarchy, born of sloth and cupidity, strong enough to dethrone this fair queen, and like Zenobia in the triumphal car of Aurelian, lead her in mockery through the streets of foreign capitals, an image of the vanity of pretensions to fitness for freedom and self-government?

All this was involved in the fearful controversy. And it was a fearful struggle, engaging every thought, energy, and affection of our loyal citizens, straining every nerve and muscle, arousing every hope and fear, testing every principle and feeling; calling the attention of our people, as never before, to the sacred functions of government, the costly nature of citizenship, the worthlessness of private wealth without public protection, and the inestimable value of peace, concord, and manhood. These were among the important elements of the conflict which, though sharp and severe, proved, doubtless, our salvation. It wakened us from our stupor, interrupted our private pursuits and cupidities seriously enough to call us to duty and lead to sacrifice, always salutary, of property and private plans, of ease and comfort, for the cause of the national weal.

It must not be forgotten that we fought not against organized slavery, but against the ideas which made slavery possible; against contempt for man; against an overvaluation of external possessions in comparison with internal qualities; of wealth, place, and luxury, as weighed with intelligence, virtue, and worth.

And therefore we came out of the war victorious, with the lost sovereignty of the Republic restored, with the capacity of our people for self-government vindicated, and in some good degree with a regenerated nation. In that strife was generated a sentiment of nationality which showed that loyalty to an idea is definite and powerful as loyalty to a throne. It revealed that the nation has an ideal character, a representative value; that its glory springs not from vast extent, populousness, power or wealth, but from the unquestioned dominion of ideas.

At the same time it also proffered a grand opportunity not only to restore but to permanently extend our national idea. It seemed the only hope of fulfilling the promises of the immortal Declaration, and of verifying the hopes of our immortal founders. We learned that a nation truly lives only when it unfolds its specific ideas and lives according to its original type. When it fails to do this it dies. The elementary principles of our government are *liberty* and *unity*. Liberty is the first fact—liberty resting not upon a distinction of race, a claim of territory or hereditary privileges, not even upon political traditions or compacts of any sort, but directly upon the primal rights of man. Unity is the other fact— unity binding and cementing all the people into one grand organization of social and national life. These ideas entwined with the very root of the Republic, running into every limb, and shooting into every fibre, bind us to the recognition of human brotherhood, to sympathy with liberty wherever it struggles, and to unflinching opposition to whatever crushes the rights, hinders the development, or denies the essential humanity of man.

The voice of war summoned us back to our original ideal, and taught us that whatever may be our prejudice against race, section, or policy, we are to look at them in the light of our own principles. Liberty and unity, one and inseparable; that was the marriage vow and *that alone* can be the marriage bond. The inward verifying principles of our government must be in sympathy with liberty; its attitude must be respect for liberty; the spread of its domain must be under the sanctions and for the ends of liberty; for this, more than all things else, gives glory to our charter and renown to our history. And the vindication of the sovereignty of this principle was the first grand issue of the war; an issue wrought out by the patriot heroes of the land pledging heart, brain, and hand—nay, even life itself—to the service of keeping our country true to its mission and obedient to its primal idea.

On such a mount of vision as we have reached this day in the opening of the second century of our historic life, where the tumult of war is hushed, the air is still, and the clouds, though not wholly scattered, are arched with the gracious bow of promise, we look back over the intervening years and recall the memory of our founders and heroic defenders—of the earlier and later sacrifices to liberty

—names not born to die. We recall the venerated Father of his Country, the first great American, too honest to be bought with foreign gold or bribed with a kingly crown; a name that never fails to touch the deepest springs of reverence and pride. We remember the list of early worthies—John Adams, with his patriotic vigor; the magnetic genius of Quincy and the invincible chivalry of Warren; the serene wisdom of Franklin and the unconquerable energy of Samuel Adams; Jefferson with his speculative audacity and Hancock with his resolute patriotism; Hamilton, with youthful but profound and lucid wisdom; Jay with his prudent analysis and Madison with his elegant research; Henry Otis and Rutledge, with their entrancing symphony of eloquence; Webster, massive and grand, the expounder and defender of the Constitution; Clay, genial, brilliant, fascinating; beside the long roll of honor from Sumter to Petersburg—the chivalrous Ellsworth, whose mysteriously shadowed face deepened his boyish beauty; the knightly Winthrop, radiant with young genius and wreathed with the choicest offerings of poesy and song; the bravehearted Lyon, who wrenched victory from the fangs of fate; the eloquent Baker, whose golden lips were sealed in death that his spirit might speak to all generations; the sage and soldier, the world-renowned Mitchell, who vacated his studio among the stars that he might wield the sword of liberty; Sheridan, animate with a daring chivalry that organizes victory out of defeat; the gallant Logan, easily among the first of our citizen soldiery, brave as he was true—adding to his military renown an ideal character in which was shown the beauty of goodness; the mighty Ulysses, whose colossal greatness forbids that we should classify his name with Cæsar, Hannibal, or Napoleon—simple, calm and commanding, unconquerable in war, invincible in peace, with practical sagacity as a statesman. How enviable his fame! He conquered the foes of his country with his sword; he won them to loyalty with his heart. What loving sympathy! What generous magnanimity! How loyal in his friendship, how brave in his fidelity! With what courage he held death still with one hand while with the other he wrote the history of his army's triumph! And how the world sobbed at his death. Royal hands placed a wreath upon his bier. Confederate generals, who contested with him many a hard-fought field, with sorrowful hearts and tearful eyes followed him to the grave, and to-morrow no State will forget to send floral tributes to his tomb; and thus North and South are cemented in perpetual unity, as the boys in blue and the boys in gray fling a bridge of roses across the bloody chasm.

Time would fail me to recall the name of Seward, the wise Secretary, skilled in the arts of diplomacy, who never despaired of the Republic; Sumner, the honorable Senator, who, as a scholar, statesman and orator, shone so brightly among men of renown—

unstained and pure in his patriotic devotion; the invincible Stanton, bearing the stress of his country's struggle on his great brain till it broke, and the long array of fallen braves who have gone down to their graves with the benediction of mankind upon them. But we must not forget—we cannot forget—another precious name. It brings to us a man of extraordinary mould, rugged in limb and strong; his countenance scarred with seams of patient thought, yet calm and tranquil, with a lambent glory resting upon it as if he had come from some mount of holy communion; his voice sonorous as the notes of a clarion, yet pathetic and kindly, though, like Moses, slow of speech; his complexion clear, the sign of purity in an age of grossness, and temperance in an age of excess; his bearing dignified, though neither haughty nor graceful; a skilled captain, a fine lawyer, an illustrious statesman, magnanimous in good fortune, unruffled in disaster; a patriot whom no ingratitude could alienate; a citizen whose sense of justice probed his own failings to the quick while it flung the mantle of its charity over the error of others. His only fault seemed an excess of virtue. If sometimes irresolute, it was only because he was loyal to truth and faithful to duty. If he failed in sagacity, it was only because his lofty purity could not realize the perfidy of others. Without signal genius, culture, or learning, he was faithful, sympathetic, and conscientious—his will so earnest, his heart so truthful, his hands so pure, that he bore across the stormy wilderness of fear, and through mounting seas of blood, the civil constitution, which is to the nation its consecrated ark. Living in times of great peril, opulent with great opportunities, working with instruments manifold and mighty, such as had never been entrusted to man before, and never so nobly used, it was his pre-eminent privilege to reveal his character in the work that made the dissevered nation a unit, and to make the principles through which it won its highest glory supreme in the confidence of his countrymen, as well as in the respect and admiration of the world.

We remember him as the Hebrews remember Moses, for he was our deliverer. His name has become a household word. A whole race sing it by the cradles of their children. It is shrined in the heart of all races. It has become the watchword of freedom, the synonym of manly character. Having given intellect, energy, ambition to the service of his country and his kind, he has made humanity more hopeful and the world more free, and to-day he stands in the highest niche of the historic temple, unrivaled and alone.

To-day the lingering mists of partisan prejudice may hang heavy clouds upon the glory of his fame, but when they shall dissolve in the flow of time, and the muse of history shall come to make up the list of her worthies, she shall put Moses for the Hebrew, Phocion for the Greek, Hampden for England, Fayette for France, Washington as the earliest flower of our civilization, and opening a fresh unstained page she shall record the life of one who embodied the nation's highest principles and noblest character, the bright consummate fruitage of American institutions; the patriot and prophet of a new era, the statesman, the liberator, the martyr and the man—the illustrious Lincoln.

And surely, while the sacred dust of these men sleep, in our soil, liberty shall not perish, and the Republic shall stand with her glory undimmed and her power unbroken.

> "They never fail who die
> In a great cause; the block may soak their gore,
> Their heads may sodden in the sun, their limbs
> Be strung to city gates and castle walls,
> But still their spirits walk abroad; though years
> Elapse, and others share as dark a doom,
> They but augment the deep of sweeping thoughts
> Which overpower all others, and conduct
> The world at last to freedom."

Other issues were also secured, visible not only in an unbroken nationality, but in the re-animation of the world's confidence in the security, the resources and mighty energy of the principle of popular government, in the quickening of the people of the Old World to an assertion of their long-suppressed rights. It was, therefore, for man, for thee, O Liberty! that we waged the terrible contest, that thy sacred privileges might be secured against the apathy of the free and prosperous, and the schemes of the despotic, for generations unborn. It was for

Europe, for Asia, for Africa, for the race, that we fought and conquered. And the result is the ascendancy and rapidly-approaching signs of freedom in all nations. A French statesman exclaimed: "A new society is in existence, called Democratic. In one half of Europe it is already sovereign. It will be in the other half to-morrow."

Thus a social energy is at work that liberates and expands. It opens the self-occupied understanding with ideas of universal brotherhood, through common sufferings and hopes. It flashes a wave of light on the race, which spreads forever and brightens as it spreads. Every oppressed people feels and responds to the impulse. Foreign despots realize the power, and proffer such concessions as will keep popular discontent this side of revolution. The tendency to the fullest liberty of thought and the recognition of the rights of man pervades the nations. The new wine is bursting the rotten bottles of hereditary privilege. Royalty is forced to repair its ragged robes, which the people are ever rending, but the Sartor Resartus has to do his patching with popular suffrage and constitutional government—some fresh-woven bit from American looms.

The armies of Freedom are on the march, and they are allied armies, before whose coming the empires of the Old World are shaken with terror. Victory to one gives prestige and confidence to all. To-day the English monarchy is convulsed throughout all the dominion of the beautiful Queen.

France, the centre of Europe's proudest civilization, often thrown into political spasms, has at last established the Republic, with some hope of its stability. Spain, haughty in her pride, and imperial in her intolerance, responds to the ringing appeals of Castelar, who gathers his inspiration from our history, and will some day be free alike from civil tyranny and priestly domination. The great German family has struggled into unity, brought Teutonic Christianity to the front, and many of her best statesmen and brightest scholars long for free institutions Italy—land of poetry, painting, music, and sculpture—land of bright-skied states—has accomplished her unity and achieved a freedom which includes suffrage nearly universal, the *habeas corpus*, liberty of religious speech that even discusses the impossibility of Peter's primacy under the shadow of the Vatican, and establishes free schools in which the Word of God is read without fear or molestation. Greece, the native home of eloquence and song, with her wondrous creations of beauty, has in these later days elected her own ruler. Russia, mighty empire of the north, an autocratic power, untrammelled by either constitution or law, relaxes her rigid iron grasp, manumits her serfs, and seeks the education of the innumerable tribes throbbing in her breast; and while the imperial power still extends over all a dark, impenetrable canopy, beneath its shadow there is individual liberty and local self-government, with a restless yearning that menaces the throne, and through patient waiting and much suffering promises the Republic by and by—at least a liberal constitutional monarchy, with representative institutions.

Thus liberty, like living seed, when planted, vivifies, expands, develops, and brings forth abundant fruit. And wherever it grows Despotism withers and dies; Democracy blooms and lives to reign as Queen of the Nations. Under her sway autocracy and caste find their doomsday. Partial privileges, unfraternal principalities and powers perish. An era of enlightened national government dawns upon mankind; for despite the evil passions and entrenched abuses which surround us, the times are pregnant with great hopes. The old foundations of error, inequality, and superstition, usually anchored in adamant, are broken loose. The iron of bad customs and stolid usage, of fixed wrong and stereotyped injustice, is all a fluid mass, melted in the fire of the world's contests. Men's minds are awake, sensitive, plastic. New and nobler ideas of humanity break forth with the emancipated millions, who drop their chains and loosen ours. The rights, the capacities, the hopes of mankind are all singing hosannas. A grand epoch has broken upon the world—an epoch that redeems us from low purposes and grovelling aims, and that should lift us into living sympathy with the grandeur of the ideas, the tendencies and the prophecies incarnated in the historic development of the times.

Brothers, the trumpet of God is sounding. It is not the bugle-call to battle. The roar of cannon and the rattle of musketry have ceased. The sabre and the bayonet flash only on parade. The bivouac, the camp, the march, are only a dream. The battalions hear no more the hoarse "Forward!" The shattered and glorious banners which you followed, and which we love so well, are carefully folded in legislative halls. The grass grows green over the soldier's lonely grave, and the bitter moans of sorrow mellow into a song of sadness. The conflict of arms is over, but the conflict of ideas is not over, nor the trials of the people. The field is changed, and now in the work-shop, the home, and at the Capitol—through the press, on the platform, and in the pulpit—we must insist upon the maintenance of the peace for which our countrymen so nobly fought and so bravely died. We must seek to elevate the intellectual spirit of the nation and deepen the channel of its moral life. We are called upon by the sacred memories of this day, in view of our needs and auspicious hopes, to cherish a lofty faith in the Republic, and to cause the nation to draw its nutriment and derive its impulse from the knowledge and love of the ideal America, as yet but partially reflected in our institutions or the general mind of the people. Thus quickened, it will become both pure and practical. We must have courage to meet our difficulties. We must remember that we have outgrown the past and that we have entered upon a new and high national life. There need be no rancor nor needless recrimination. We must be inspired with hope. We must stand together. We must forget and forgive. We must rub out old animosities and take a fresh, unstained parchment fit to receive the lines and lessons of a later time. We must carry hopeful hearts and cheerful brows. We must fill the veins of education and the organization of industry with the spirit of liberty. We must mould the life of the nation by the force of great moral ideas, and rule through the royalty of principle that can never be discrowned. Let them have an unquestioned light of supremacy and create a dynasty of moral forces that shall be supreme. Let intelligence, freedom, law, religion—the four immovable pillars of communal morality—stand forever the basis of our institutions and the guide of our Rulers in their administration. Then shall we be able to show forth the glory of our land—of the new age—and to meet the urgent and precious invitations of this new epoch.

They tell us it is a degenerate age—an age of materialism, given to pelf and plunder. It is not so. Men as knightly and brave as ever graced heroic age still live, and would willingly die for the defence of the Republic. The American spirit still survives. The fires of patriotism are fanned into a vestal flame; honor thrives, and noble characters adorn the high places of the land. Loyalty has not perished. Myriads of heroic spirits look upon the nation's ensign and cry, "My country's flag ; emblem of a nation that covers half a continent ; hope of a people that loves liberty ; blazonry of the rights of man, before thee I bow ; the symbol of a nation's glory, to thee my allegiance, for thee my prayers ; and if, in bearing thee through the fiery storms and deadly hail, my blood should flow in a crimson tide, under thy starry folds would I find my grave."

Oh, Soldier ! look not back to the fearful struggle alone ; meditate not upon thy scars, so honorably won, but look forward to the fruit of your sacrifices ! Oh, Patriot ! mourn not the desolation of the past. Lift up thine eyes and behold the temple of Freedom—a Nation's Home, paved with the lively stones of great principles—its arches resounding with the songs of freedom and festooned with flags torn and rent in battle ; its ceiling resplendent with the ever-burning stars and ribbed with the unfading stripes of that banner which has become the symbol of hope to oppressed millions. See its windows stained with the blood of martyred youth, the pride and glory of their generation. Bow at its altars, and you shall read the original Declaration of our Fathers bound in with the Book of Life, and find it a New Testament for the political future of all nations. Around you are gathered the arts, sciences, and industries of an earnest people, which have become conscious instruments of public intelligence, common happiness, and social good ; you may see wealth consecrated to usefulness, genius anointed with faith, beauty bending in prayer, and inclination wedded with duty. Into this glorious temple a teeming agriculture brings her yellow sheaves, rejoicing that she may banquet on her virgin acres the world's hungry millions. The mountains unlock their wealth and heap their richest treasure against the monolithic pillars. Nay, greater than these material glories, we behold the tribes of the Old World—of Europe, of the Flowery Kingdom, of India, and the Isles of the Sea—filing into the wide portals, their banners written all over with gratitude and hope, seeking to inaugurate that royal age when the races shall meet together and dwell in peace ; when men of all nations shall stand side by side as brothers in the majesty of awakened conscience, with large hearts, filled with loyalty and love, unblenched before the pride of power, with faith untiring and heroism that fails not amidst hazard and hardship, and is ever radiant with the truth—men who shall put knowledge below culture, culture below character, and Christianity over all, as the chief hope of humanity. Then we may exclaim with the poet:

"Lo, another age is rising—in the coming years I see
Hopes and promises of blessing, light, and love, and liberty;
All the good the past hath garnered, all the present yet hath won,
Fade before the glorious future, like the stars before the sun.
Truth, for every eye is shining in the fullness of that day,
Joy and hope, decended angels, rest, no more to pass away;
Freedom comes and lifts the captive from the dungeon of his woe.

And all streams of mortal being deeper, purer, sweeter flow.
There, the thunder of the captains and their shoutings die away,
Melting into love's sweet music, like the darkness into day;
And the chorus of the Nations, as the rolling years increase,
Rises in harmonious numbers, peaceful, to the Prince of Peace."

www.ingramcontent.com/pod-product-compliance
Lightning Source LLC
Chambersburg PA
CBHW021729220426
43662CB00008B/769